water,
wind,
earth
&*fire*

For too many centuries, too many Christians have been taught that a deep reverence for the beauty of nature is incompatible with sincere faith. Christine Valters Paintner's *Water, Wind, Earth, and Fire* thus comes as both a blessing and a gift. Not only is her writing as beautiful as the symbolism she describes, but her wide knowledge of scripture, patristic writing, the mystical life of the saints, and contemporary spiritual poetry makes the reading of this book an inspiring and rejuvenating adventure.

Paula Huston
Author of *The Holy Way*

Christine Valters Paintner invites us—with inspiring words and examples—to dive deep into the elemental universe, and encounter there the Mystery that hides in all things. She writes out of the Christian tradition, but her message is as universal as the elements themselves.

Chet Raymo
Author of *When God Is Gone, Everything Is Holy*

Amid the current profusion of spirituality-and-nature books, *Water, Wind, Earth, and Fire* is a rare treasure: a deeply Christian book that also draws us more deeply into contemplation of and relationship with nature. This fine work of spiritual wisdom and guidance offers to both individuals and groups a companion for all seasons. It can soothe at night, enliven in the morning, kindle the human spirit during the day, and at all times serve as a reminder of the abiding presence of the Creator Spirit, which is the spirit of Christ on earth and among us.

Jane Redmont
Author of *When in Doubt, Sing*

water, wind, earth & fire

The *Christian Practice*

of

Praying with the *Elements*

CHRISTINE VALTERS PAINTNER

SORIN BOOKS  Notre Dame, Indiana

Copyright acknowledgments for excerpts used in this book are detailed in the Sources section on pages 143–149, which is a continuation of this copyright page.

www.sorinbooks.com

ISBN-10 1-933495-22-7   ISBN-13 978-1-933495-22-4

Cover and text design by Brian C. Conley.

cover art © iStockphoto

Printed and bound in the United States of America.

Library of Congress Cataloging-in-Publication Data
Paintner, Christine Valters.
  Water, wind, earth, and fire : the Christian practice of praying with the elements / Christine Valters Paintner.
      p. cm.
  Includes bibliographical references.
  ISBN-13: 978-1-933495-22-4 (pbk.)
  ISBN-10: 1-933495-22-7 (pbk.)
  1. Prayer—Christianity. 2. Nature—Religious aspects—Christianity. 3. Four elements (Philosophy)—Miscellanea. I. Title.
  BV227.P35 2010
  248.3'2—dc22
                                    2009043975

To Abbess Petunia and former Abbott Duke (1996–2006)
whose four-legged wisdom has taught me about the
profound mysteries and graces of the natural world.
They have each revealed a face of God in their
being just who they were created to be.

Contents

Acknowledgments

I am profoundly grateful for the whole community of support present behind the writing of this book. An abundance of thanks are due to the following people:

my beloved husband John, whose unfailing support of my writing has been an essential gift in my life.

Kayce Stevens Hughlett, one of my wonderful work partners and a dear friend, who read an early version of this manuscript and offered great feedback and encouragement.

Betsey Beckman, my other teaching partner and close friend, with whom I first explored the four elements in a ritual and prayer context in our "Awakening the Creative Spirit" training program in the expressive arts.

Sister Laura Swan, who so kindly connected me with Ave Maria Press because of her own very positive experience with them and who has been a great encouragement in the writing life.

Sister Lucy Wynkoop, who is a mentor, friend, collaborator, and wonderful source of support.

my Benedictine Oblate community, who continually reminds me what it means to live a holy ordinary life.

Charles Skriner and Bob Hamma, editors at Ave Maria Press, for their most gracious and enthusiastic support.

my parents, who took their young daughter to walk in the woods, hike in the mountains, and play along the seashore. These childhood experiences were the seeds for this work.

Introduction

All praise be Yours, my God, through Brothers Wind and Air,
And fair and stormy, all the weather's moods,
By which You cherish all that You have made.

All praise be Yours, my God, through Sister Water,
So useful, humble, precious, and pure.

All praise be Yours, my God, through Brother Fire,
Through whom You brighten up the night.
How beautiful he is, how gay!
Full of power and strength.

All praise be Yours, my God, through Sister Earth, our mother,
Who feeds us in her sovereignty and produces
Various fruits and colored flowers and herbs.

—St. Francis of Assisi

Nature as a Book of Revelation

How necessary it is for monks to work in the fields,
in the rain, in the sun, in the mud, in the clay, in the
wind: these are our spiritual directors and our novice-
masters. They form our contemplation. They instill
us with virtue. They make us as stable as the land we
live in.

—Thomas Merton

All things with which we deal preach to us. What is
a farm but a mute gospel? The chaff and the wheat,
weeds and plants, blight, rain, insects, sun—it is a
sacred emblem from the first furrow of spring to the
last stack which the snow of winter overtakes in the
fields.

—Ralph Waldo Emerson

Christian tradition tells us that we have received two books
of divine revelation: the book of scripture and the book of nature.
Creation itself is a sacred text through which the presence of God
is revealed to us. There is a story about the hermit Antony, who
lived in the desert of Egypt in the third to fourth centuries. When
he was asked once by a philosopher what he would do if one day he
could no longer read scripture, Antony replied simply: "My book, sir
philosopher, is the nature of created things, and it is always on hand
when I wish to read it." In this brief exchange we witness the essential role of the natural world in forming Christian awareness and
practice from ancient times.

Celtic Christian tradition especially has developed this understanding of the natural world as a window onto the divine; nature is considered to be an essential source of revelation about God. This is in large part why Celtic Christian practices and wisdom are being reclaimed with great enthusiasm in our contemporary world. People are hungry for ways to reconnect with creation in meaningful and prayerful ways.

This primary connection to creation is rooted in the example of Jesus himself, who expressed many of his teachings through parables, those profound stories that reveal to us the nature of God and God's Reign. Much of the language Jesus used is earth-based, rooted in metaphors of seed, fruit, and harvest with which his listeners would have identified. His ministry also centers around elemental places, such as feasting at the table on the gifts of the earth, his appearance on the mountain as a place of transfiguration, his encounters at the well, and his own baptism in the River Jordan, as just a few examples.

In the opening quotation to this section, Thomas Merton is referring to monks, but he is essentially speaking to all of us who yearn for a closer relationship to God. The wind and rain, sun and mud are representations of the four elements of air, fire, water, and earth. As Merton indicates, they can act as spiritual directors or guides to help us along the sacred journey. The qualities of these elements offer an invitation to us to pray with them, so that we might come to know what they reveal about the nature of God and our own spiritual unfolding.

The Four Elements: Wind, Water, Fire, Earth

I arise today
Through the strength of heaven;
Light of the sun,
Splendor of fire,
Speed of lightning,

Swiftness of the wind,
Depth of the sea,
Stability of the earth,
Firmness of the rock.

—St. Patrick

An element is the basic or essential constituent of something. Ancient philosophies identified four elements that make up the universe and explain patterns in nature. Interest in the four elements can be traced back as far as the Greek philosopher Empedocles in the fifth century BC. The Greek classical elements are earth, water, air, and fire; and these are also found in other cultures, including Eastern Indian and Japanese. The ancients did not believe these elements comprised the *literal* basis of matter. Rather, they found a *symbolic* quality in each of the elements that expresses something none of the others could: the grounded quality of earth, the fluidity of water, the passion of fire, and the blowing of the wind. As we will see in this book, each of these symbolic qualities opens up to us a dimension of God as well.

Christianity inherited the Greek worldview, including the four elements, and integrated these ideas into its own theological system. Both the Hebrew and Christian Scriptures are filled with images of God rooted in the elements of the natural world. The Psalms especially use the language of earth, water, fire, and wind to describe God, to give insight into the multiplicity of God's qualities, and to celebrate a God who can be found within the matrix of creation. In the Christian scriptures, we find the four elements represented in multiple ways. The Spirit is represented as both wind and fire. The living water of baptism is a central symbol for our self-understanding as members of the Christian community. The communion feast springs from the gifts of bread and wine, earth's nourishment.

In addition to scripture, we have an enormous treasure of writings from the Christian mystics, spanning nearly two thousand years. You will find their voices and wisdom in these pages. Those who celebrated God through the images of the elements include

St. Francis of Assisi, St. Teresa of Avila, St. Benedict of Nursia, St. Ignatius of Loyola, and Hildegard of Bingen, as well as some of our more modern mystical voices, including Pierre Teilhard de Chardin, Thomas Merton, and many others.

These four elements, in addition to becoming integral to Christian symbolism, also have been important for a variety of nature-based spiritual traditions and practices. Thus, as Pope Benedict XVI (then Cardinal Ratzinger) wrote in 1987, seeing the water used in baptism, for example, as cosmic matter "forms a link between the Christian faith and the religions of the nations, which, as cosmic religions, seek God in the elements of the world and are actually on his trail, albeit from a distance" (p. 29, *Principles of Catholic Theology*).

The elements also are held in tension with each other in terms of the qualities they represent. We typically consider fire and water as opposites and earth and air as opposites. This tension invites us to also pray with the elements toward a reconciliation of the paradoxes of the world and toward a union of the opposing forces within us in our soul's quest for integration and wholeness.

Finally, the fact that the elements are four in number is also of importance. The number four is significant in nature, especially the four seasons of the year and the four quarters or directions (east, west, north, and south). Four is also a sacred number within Christian and Hebrew traditions: the four rivers in the garden of Eden (Gn 2:10), four faces on the cherubs of Ezekiel (man, lion, bull, and eagle) corresponding to the four directions (Ez 1:10), the four corners and fours winds of the earth in Revelation (7:1), the four-walled New Jerusalem (Rv 21:7), and of course, the four gospels.

Connections to the Four Directions

I saw four angels standing at the four corners of the earth.

—Revelation 7:1

The four elements and the four directions can help further illuminate the qualities of the particular elements. Throughout the chapters of this book, I will draw on the connections made by the Cherokee peoples, who link air with the direction of the east, fire with the south, water with the west, and earth with the north.

We may tend to think of honoring the directions as primarily a Native American or pagan practice. However, we find this directional awareness rooted in Christianity as well. In the Orthodox tradition, the four directions are a concrete part of the liturgical action. For example, during the "Great Blessing of Waters" on the Feast of Epiphany, the celebrant immerses a cross in the holy water three times and then sprinkles water in each of the four directions of the world. In Jewish practice, on each day of the nine-day harvest festival of Sukkoth (Sukkah meaning booths or huts), palm branches, myrtle, and willow are bound together and waved in the four directions to symbolize God, who dwells everywhere, as well as the unity of people across the globe and with creation.

In determining the number of gospels to be four, St. Irenaeus, a second-century bishop of Lyon in Roman Gaul, declared Mark, Matthew, Luke, and John the only gospels that Christians should read. For Irenaeus, the number four was extremely important in light of the four directions and four winds, and so he reasoned that there should be four separate gospels as well. The Christian cross itself symbolizes the four directions and the desire to spread the Word to the four corners of the earth.

The direction of the east became associated with the resurrection, in part because of this passage from Matthew: "For just as lightning comes from the east and is seen as far as the west, so will the coming of the Son of Man be" (24:27). The east is associated with the dawning of the new day. Many churches are built with their altars facing east, and cemeteries are often oriented in this direction as well. People are then buried with their feet facing east so that when they rise they will be facing God. A popular hymn for Advent invites us to face east:

People, look East, the time is near
of the crowning of the year.
Make your house fair as you are able,
trim the hearth and set the table.
People look East and sing today,
Love, the Guest, is on the way!

—Eleanor Farjeon

Invitation to Elemental Prayer

God created the world out of its elements to the
glory of the divine name. God strengthened it with
the wind, connected it to the stars and enlightened
it by them, and filled it with all manner of creatures.
God then surrounded and fulfilled humankind in the
world with all things and gave them a tremendous
power, so that all creation would support them in all
things. The whole nature should serve them, so that
they can live with it, because humankind cannot live
or survive without nature.

—Hildegard of Bingen

When we recognize ourselves as a part of the earth community, as the scriptures and mystics have encouraged us to do for centuries, then we begin to see the profound mystery at work in the depths of our own souls as the same sacred mystery at work in the natural world. Being present to the gifts of creation helps to give us insight into paths for our own spiritual growth and into the ways in which God is present to us.

This book is designed to be an accompaniment and guide for ongoing prayer and times of retreat. It is an offering—one window among many—into cultivating a more intimate and contemplative relationship to God through the natural world. Each of the elements offers us a unique energy or way of understanding the sacred: water flows and cleanses; the earth roots us and nourishes us; fire represents the burning of love and passion; and wind expresses freedom, breath, and unpredictability. Each chapter that follows will break open the multiple qualities each element expresses and offer ways to pray with these qualities and grow in our relationship to the divine Source pulsing at the heart of the world.

By bringing the four elements into our prayer, we can cultivate two primary connections: First, by rooting our prayer in connection with the elements, we begin to forge an awareness of how much we are a part of creation and share in the earth's elements. We may begin to experience ourselves as a part of the matrix of the natural world and as part of the same creation as other of God's creatures.

Second, in opening ourselves to the metaphors that the elements offer us for how God works in the world, we discover a God who dwells at the heart of all living things, who sustains and transforms creation moment by moment, and who is an indispensable presence in the world. Reflecting on the nature of God in connection with the four elements helps to strengthen our sense of the sacred presence in our midst and reveals a God whose immanence shimmers through creation.

This book, then, encourages your spiritual path and practice to be fully embodied through this wondrous world with which we have been gifted. This means practicing gratitude for the abundant gifts of God symbolized in the elements and rooting prayer in a sense of all of creation as a great sacrament or as a window onto the holy. In allowing the qualities of the elements to become part of our prayer, we can recognize God's active work in creation since the very beginning of time.

Contemplative, Ascetic, and Prophetic Responses

> The beauty and grandeur of nature touches each
> one of us. From panoramic vistas to the tiniest living
> form, nature is a constant source of wonder and awe.
> It is also a continuing revelation of the divine.
>
> —Canadian Conference of Catholic Bishops

In the letter referenced above, the Canadian Catholic Bishops published a moving document that describes the threefold nature of our responsibility to the environment, rooted in the Christian tradition: the contemplative response, the ascetic response, and the prophetic response.

The contemplative response is an invitation to stand in awe of the beauty and wonder of the created world. In the rush of our lives we rarely have time to contemplate anything, much less nature. Yet, taking time to be fully present to the world around us can expand us through awe and a sense of gratitude. We can begin to cherish such beauty and long to ensure its protection. In cultivating a contemplative relationship to nature, our hearts are transformed, and we can begin to live in more conscious and life-giving ways.

Asceticism does not ring well in modern ears. Essentially a lifestyle based in abstinence from selected activities or things, it may call to mind the early Christian monks who lived austere lives of strict renunciation. With our contemporary understanding of psychology, we can appreciate the importance of pleasure to a healthy life. Yet there is still great wisdom to be discovered in the conscious choice to live with less. There is a profound gift in the invitation to ask ourselves what the things that distract us from God are. The ascetic response invites us to consider restraining ourselves from the rampant consumerism of our times and to cultivate a *new* asceticism—one rooted in adjusting our lifestyle choices to limit consumption, waste, and pollution.

The prophetic response invites us to consider the ecological imperative as a justice issue. Poverty and pollution are intimately connected, as poor communities are far more likely than others to bear the brunt of environmental toxicity or to lack access to clean water supplies. Embracing the prophetic dimension of our relationship to the natural world calls us to ask questions about the source of the food we eat, the kinds of energy we use, and the pollutants created to make the products we use.

All three responses are essential to a holistic spirituality that takes seriously our place in creation. The heart of this book, however, rests in offering you resources and tools primarily for cultivating your contemplative response to the world. The main focus will be to engage each of the traditional four natural elements—wind, fire, water, and earth—as windows into the tremendous gifts creation offers to us as insight into God's nature and ourselves through the symbols of the elements. Each chapter will focus on one of the elements and is further divided into sections to illuminate different dimensions of each element from a perspective rooted in the Christian tradition. Each of these sections offers relevant quotations from scripture, mystics, and poets, a reflection to invite you to contemplate more deeply the spiritual life from the perspective of the element, questions for your prayerful reflection, and suggestions for ways to practice this contemplative response to nature in your time of meditation or prayer.

Cultivating Our Relationship to Nature

Nature to a saint is sacramental. If we are children
of God, we have a tremendous treasure in Nature. In
every wind that blows, in every night and day of the
year, in every sign of the sky, in every blossoming
and in every withering of the earth, there is a real
coming of God to us if we will simply use our starved
imagination to realize it.

—Oswald Chambers

All my life has been a relearning to pray—a
letting go of incantational magic, petition, and the
vain repetition "Me Lord, me," instead watching
attentively for the light that burns at the center of
every star, every cell, every living creature, every
human heart.

—Chet Raymo

Ever since I was very young I have loved the natural world. I grew up in the heart of New York City but regularly sought out Central Park as a connection to nature in the midst of the city. In the summers, my family would travel to my father's native Austria and spend time hiking in the Vienna woods and the Tyrolean mountains. Even though my parents were not religious people, as a small child I had a profound sense of that stunning, humbling mountainous landscape as a window onto something much larger and more powerful than myself that I would eventually come to name God.

I now live in Seattle, where we are surrounded by mountain chains, waterways, and forests. For many people in the Pacific Northwest, a region known for being "unchurched," being in nature is a primary experience of the holy. Trees, mountains, and oceans sing of the sacred dimension of the world present to us in their natural splendor and beauty. Hiking and kayaking offer moments of profound communion with the natural world in ways that reveal God's presence as abundant.

Chet Raymo's words opening this section invite us into a different relationship to prayer. We are called to move beyond the prayers of asking for blessings on our lives and to become fully present to the gifts and energy of the world around us. We are invited to join in and participate in the prayer of praise already happening within creation. Psalm 96 celebrates this dynamic at work: "Let the heavens be glad and the earth rejoice; let the sea roar and all that fills it; let the field exult, and everything in it. Then shall all the trees of the forest sing for joy before the Lord" (vv. 11–13). We can join in those choirs singing gratitude to the God who sustains us moment by moment.

I invite you in the pages that follow to open your hearts to the sacred presence in nature and experience yourself as deeply connected to the whole earth community of which we are all a part. This book encourages meaningful connections between the inner spiritual journey and the outer sacred world of creation. Thomas Becknell, in the introduction to his book *Of Earth and Sky*, writes: "What Nature provides us are not models for choosing, but models of being—vibrant examples of things living as they were meant to be." Our Christian tradition offers us a wealth of riches and reflections to help us understand the gifts nature offers us to bring us closer to God. There is a wealth of imagery thematically gathered here together to support you in your spiritual journey. May you be blessed by the heart of God pulsing through all of creation.

Deep peace of the running wave to you,
of water flowing, rising and falling,
sometimes advancing, sometimes receding. . . .
May the stream of your life flow unimpeded!
Deep peace of the running wave to you!

Deep peace of the flowing air to you,
which fans your face on a sultry day,
the air which you breathe deeply, rhythmically,
which imparts to you energy, consciousness, life.
Deep peace of the flowing air to you!

Deep peace of the quiet earth to you, who, herself unmoving,
harbors the movements
and facilitates the life of the ten thousand creatures,
while resting contented, stable, tranquil.
Deep peace of the quiet earth to you!

Deep peace of the shining stars to you,
which stay invisible till darkness falls
and disclose their pure and shining presence
beaming down in compassion on our turning world.
Deep peace of the shining stars to you!

—CELTIC PRAYER

chapter one

Brother Wind

All praise be Yours, my God, through Brothers Wind and Air,
And fair and stormy, all the weather's moods,
By which You cherish all that You have made.

—St. Francis of Assisi

Deep peace of the flowing air to you,
which fans your face on a sultry day,
the air which you breathe deeply, rhythmically,
which imparts to you energy, consciousness, life.
Deep peace of the flowing air to you!

—Celtic Prayer

Wind and Creation

Let me seek, then, the gift of silence, and poverty,
and solitude, where everything I touch is turned into
prayer: where the sky is my prayer, the birds are my
prayer, the wind in the trees is my prayer, for God is
in all.

—Thomas Merton

In the beginning, when God created the heavens and
    the earth,
the earth was a formless void and darkness covered
    the face of the deep,
while a wind from God swept over the face of the
    waters.

—Genesis 1:1–2

Be still deadening North wind;
South wind come, you that waken love,
Breathe through my garden,
Let its fragrance flow,
And the beloved will feed among the flowers.

—St. John of the Cross

The secret life of Me breathes in the wind
And holds all things together soulfully.

—Hildegard of Bingen

You ride on the wings of the wind,
You make the winds your messengers.

—Psalm 104:3–4

Wind is the only one of the four elements that is invisible. The gift of air lacks any discernible form or color or texture, but it makes everything else come alive both literally, as in the gift of life-giving breath, and figuratively, as in the buffeting of things by the wind's power. In Genesis we are told that the mighty wind was present at the very beginning of creation. Wind is air in motion caused by differences in atmospheric pressure. We measure the wind or air by the effect it has on other things, such as the sail of a boat billowing, the treasure of a cooling breeze on a warm day, the gentle bending and bowing of grass in a field, the steady rhythm of our own breathing, or the powerful effects of a strong storm knocking down trees and power lines. Air is also the medium of sound-waves and thus of language and communication. It is connected to voice, our ability to speak of what is most precious to us and to communicate with others.

The metaphor of air or wind offers us a variety of ways to understand our experience of God: as life-breath, as inspiration, as enlivener, as directional guide, as powerful force, or as the current that supports flight. In this chapter you will be invited to pray with air or wind by considering a number of the wind's qualities as symbols for our relationship with God.

St. Francis, in his famous prayer that opens this book, welcomes the wind in all its manifestations and directly associates it with God's work as Creator. Brother Wind is seen as the Creator's fellow-worker, the one who cherishes, supports, strengthens, and invigorates other creatures. Franciscan author Eloi Leclerc, in his book *The Canticle of Creatures: Symbols of Union*, writes of the freedom and detachment of St. Francis's words of praise for Brother Wind:

> All its moods! In fact, for [Francis] there is no [such] thing as bad weather any longer. His brotherly feeling for the wind springs from an interior detachment and openness of soul that a man reaches only after much striving. Francis was a man of the open air, there has never been a more receptive soul than St. Francis. The context of the wind is a world open and exposed and swept by a force that will not let you rest and carries you further and further, a force

that refuses to be fettered and overturns every dividing wall and every barrier . . . we can say that the poetic celebration of the wind in all its manifestations shows a soul aspiring to open itself to Being in its entirety and to all its inspirations.

The element of wind invites us to "open our souls to Being," which means opening ourselves to a God who flows in directions we cannot predict. This element invites us to a radical posture of surrender in releasing our hold on our own plans and making room for God to blow us in the most life-giving direction. As a metaphor for God, wind reminds us that God's ways are not our ways. The invitation of wind requires of us a detachment from our own longing to control the direction of our lives and a simultaneous surrender to Spirit to allow ourselves to be carried to places of growth and newness.

Wind is also thought to be the most mobile of the elements. The movement of air and its origins and dynamics are more mysterious than those of water; and while the oceans seem deep, vast, and mysterious, they cover only a percentage of the world's surface, while air envelopes the whole globe.

As I write this chapter on air and wind, I place a feather on my prayer altar. Each morning before I begin I hold it in my hands and ask to be lifted up by the Spirit and given insight and inspiration that will take flight. I take a few moments to breathe deeply the invigorating gift of air.

In this chapter you are invited to explore the wide range of wind's expression and energy in your prayer: as life-breath, as inspiration, as directional force by allowing yourself to be carried where the wind blows, as powerful sacred presence in the midst of the whirlwind and storms of life, and as the current that lifts your wings in flight.

Getting in Touch with the Element of Wind

- Go sailing.
- Blow bubbles.
- Watch birds flying overhead.

- Lay on the cool grass and gaze at clouds drifting by.
- Fly a kite.
- On a warm summer day, take time to relish the cool breeze that refreshes.
- Light incense in your prayer space and ask that your prayers be carried up toward the heavens with the smoke that rises.
- Consider the power of a windmill.
- Roll down the windows in your car or put your top down and feel the breeze on your face, the wind through your hair.
- Support the development and use of wind energy in your community.

Life Breath

The LORD God formed man from the dust of the
   ground
and breathed into his nostrils the breath of life,
and man became a living being.

—Genesis 2:7

God is breath.

—St. Maximus the Confessor

God has given to the earth the breath which feeds
it. It is his breath that gives life to all things. And if
he were to withhold his breath, everything would
be annihilated. His breath vibrates in yours, in your

19

voice. It is the breath of God that you breathe—and
you are unaware of it.

—Theophilus of Antioch

The soul that is united and transformed in God
breathes God in God with the same divine breathing
with which God, while in her, breathes in himself.

—St. John of the Cross

When you hide your face, they are dismayed. When
you take away their breath, they die and return to
their dust. When you send forth your spirit, they are
created, and you renew the face of the earth.

—Psalm 104:29–30

In his hand is the life of every living thing, and the
breath of every human being.

—Job 12:10

While the gift of wind is mightily present in the first creation
story, another expression of this element, the gift of air or breath,
appears in a life-giving way in the second creation story. In the second chapter of Genesis we are offered the image of a transcendent
and powerful God who gathers up earth and mud and lovingly molds
each indentation, dimple, and crevice into the human person. Then
in an act of profound intimacy, God presses God's sacred lips to the
nostril opening and breathes divine spirit and life into this creature,
animating the human into a living being. Here is an expression of
God's tender immanence: God is as close to us as our very breath.
God is the sustainer of our breathing. God meets us in the place of
dust and clay from which we emerge and to which we return, and
infuses us with this life-giving, energizing connection.

Scripture tells us in many ways that it is through the gift of the Spirit that God is the animator of all living things. The Hebrew word for Spirit is *ruach,* which also means the breath of God. God breathed life into us at the moment of creation and continues to breathe into us, through us, and around us. The Sacred Source of Life blows this breath of life into *all* of creation. The great modern mystic and Jesuit Pierre Teilhard de Chardin offered the vision of the "breathing together of all things." We are connected to all of life through breath—to humans and animals, as well as to trees and plants, which breathe in the carbon dioxide we release and return oxygen to us in a harmonious exchange and dance of life.

Praying with the gift of air through attention to breath is an ancient Christian practice. One of the earliest known forms is the *Jesus prayer.* The idea behind this prayer is that we connect our conscious prayer with each breath, so that our awareness of God becomes as natural as our breathing and that we might learn to "pray without ceasing" (1 Thes 5:17). The words of this prayer said on the in-breath are "Lord Jesus Christ, Son of God," and on the out-breath, "have mercy on me, a sinner." It is also called the *Prayer of the Heart,* because we are invited to speak the words from our heart and to root our prayer in the rhythms of its beating. St. John Climacus writes, "Let the Jesus prayer cleave to your breath," and "With your breathing combine watchfulness and the name of Jesus." Elsewhere he says, "Let us live every moment in 'applying our hearts to wisdom' (Ps 90:12) as the psalmist says, continually breathing Jesus Christ, the power of God the Father and the Wisdom of God." The pursuit of wisdom, for the ancient teachers, involves practicing with the breath.

The tradition of *centering prayer* is an expression of Christian breath prayer as well. In centering prayer you choose a word or phrase that makes you more aware of God's presence, but it can also be practiced by simply being in touch with your breath and using the in and out breaths as an anchor that draws you more deeply into the presence of God.

St. Ignatius of Loyola, in his *Spiritual Exercises,* advises several methods of praying, including to "Pray According to Rhythmic Measures," which is another form of breath prayer. Ignatius writes:

"With each breath taken in or expelled, one should pray mentally, by saying a word of the Our Father, or of any other prayer which is recited. This is done in such a manner that one word of the prayer is said between one breath and another. In between these two breaths one reflects especially on the meaning of that word, or on the person to whom the prayer is being recited." The breath becomes a means by which we slow ourselves down and can begin to be really present to the words we speak in prayer.

FOR REFLECTION

- How do I experience the gift of breath?
- Where in my life do I need to breathe more deeply?
- When I pay attention to my breath, what do I become aware of in my body?

PRAYING WITH AIR AS SACRED BREATH

- As a way of entering your time of prayer, take time to get in touch with your breathing. Don't try to change the rhythm of your breath; simply notice your natural, rhythmic rise and fall. Imagine as you breathe in that God breathes life into you. As you breathe out, imagine releasing all of the distractions and worries that keep you from being fully present in prayer. See if you can just set them aside for a time. Simply spending time with your breath as a way of deepening your awareness of the God who sustains you moment by moment is enough. Take time to become aware of your breathing, and allow your heart to fill with gratitude for this most basic gift of life.

- You can practice centering prayer by using your breath as a guide to drop your awareness inward. Using the image of God's Spirit as life-giving breath, allow that image to help you to rest in God's presence as you follow your own breath into stillness.

- If you feel drawn to use words in your prayer, you might want to add the words of the Jesus prayer to your breath rhythm (in-breath: "Lord Jesus Christ, Son of God" / out-breath: "have mercy on me, a sinner"). Or use another traditional prayer that is meaningful to you, such as the Lord's Prayer. As St. Ignatius of Loyola suggested, say each word with one breath, allowing yourself to slow down and really relish the ancient words of the prayer you are saying.

- You can also create your own sacred phrase or mantra to repeat on the in-breath and out-breath. For instance, upon breathing in say, "I receive the gift of life"; upon breathing out say, "I release and surrender." Spend a few moments in silence to see if you can receive the words of your own breath-prayer, those that rise up from your heart, rather than intentionally creating it.

- Either as a closing for your time of prayer, or a prayer that stands on its own, call to mind Pierre Teilhard de Chardin's image of the "breathing together of all things." Imagine as you breathe in and out that your breath is connected in rhythm to the breath of the people you love who are also breathing in and out at this very moment. Allow your imagination to slowly expand so that you visualize your breath connecting you to all other people. Then expand again to include all living creatures. Finally, expand your vision to include trees and plant life, which offer us a mutual exchange of breath. Allow this prayer to connect you to the vast matrix of pulsing life within which we live.

Holy Inspiration

When the day of Pentecost had come, they were all
together in one place.
And suddenly from heaven there came a sound like
the rush of a violent wind,
And it filled the entire house where they were sitting.

—Acts 2:1–2

Holy Spirit,
making life alive,
moving in all things,
You are the source of all creation and beings.

Holy Spirit,
cleansing the world of every impurity,
forgiving guilt,
anointing wounds,
glistening,
You are commendable.

You are Life.
You awaken and reawaken everything that is.

—Hildegard of Bingen

This property for which the soul prays so that she
may love perfectly she here calls the breathing
of the air, because it is a most delicate touch and
feeling which the soul feels at this time in the
communication of the Holy Spirit; who, sublimely
breathing with that his divine breath, raises the soul
and informs her that she may breathe into God the
same breath of love that the Father breathes into the
Son and the Son into the Father, which is the same
Holy Spirit that they breathe into her in the said
transformation. . . . But the soul that is united and
transformed in God breathes in God into God the
same divine breath that God, being in her, breathes
into her in himself.

—St. Thérèse of Lisieux

Still the Breath Divine does move, and the breath
Divine is Love.

—William Blake

When a bird remains long on the ground it thereby
weakens its wings and its feathers grow heavy. Then
it rises, flaps its wings and swings itself up till it takes
to the air and glides into flight. The longer it flies,
the more blissfully it soars, refreshing itself, hardly
alighting on the earth to rest. So it is with the soul:
We must prepare ourselves in the same way if we
wish to come to God. We must rise on wings of
longing up to him.

—Mechtild of Magdeburg

The life-giving and sustaining breath of the Spirit is a gift at its
most fundamental level. In addition to sustaining our lives, breath
and wind also offer us the gifts of awakening and inspiration. When
a room in our home feels stuffy, we open a window to "let in some
fresh air." Making a conscious effort to breathe more deeply helps
us to feel more alert and awake. We awaken from our slumber each
morning, both literally and figuratively. The spiritual journey is a
lifetime invitation to notice the places where we have fallen asleep
and then awaken again and again—to the beauty of the world, to
the abundance of our lives, to the sacredness and dignity of each
person, to our own giftedness, to the ways we are called to share
those gifts with others, and to the power of love and kindness when
we are able to release them into the world.

The Latin word for Spirit is *spiritus* and is the same root as the
word "inspire." One of the gifts of the Spirit is inspiration—as we
breathe in life, we also breathe in new vision and possibility. The
Book of Acts tells us the story of the disciples gathered together after

Jesus' death in the upper room. At the feast of Pentecost, the Holy Spirit comes to them as both driving wind and tongues of fire. The Spirit re-awakens the disciples to their own courage and conviction. They are given the gift of tongues, which is the gift of communication. Air or breath is the medium through which we give voice to the things we believe most deeply. The Spirit breathes courage and a sense of freedom into them, necessary to go forth and offer the vision of an alternative way of being to the world. We can pray with the gift of air through awareness of its inspirational qualities. When we pray with the image of the Holy Spirit revealed at Pentecost, we can pray with the sacred gifts of renewal and awakening offered to us by God in each moment.

When I read Mechtild of Magdeburg's words about rising up "on wings of longing" to God, I am reminded of the time I spent several months in a small cottage on the water and of herons that I would often observe there. I would walk for hours along the shoreline and see these beautiful creatures standing alone. Then suddenly they would lift themselves into the air on their great wings and fly across the horizon of my vision with such grace. Every time I witnessed this scene, I would experience a connection between their wings of longing and my own. I felt myself lifted for a moment, inspired, carried higher.

The quotations above from St. Thérèse of Lisieux and the poet William Blake offer us another way we are inspired by the Spirit: God breathes love into us. The gift of the Spirit through air is creative inspiration, but just as important, it is the inspiration to grow in our love of others and ourselves. We are invited to continually open our hearts and participate in the love that flows between the three persons of the Trinity.

FOR REFLECTION

- Where in your life do you feel asleep and need to be awakened?
- Where do you need the gift of courage to help you move out of your fear?
- What is being inspired in you?

- How is the Breath of Love inviting you to open your heart?

PRAYING WITH AIR AS GIFT OF INSPIRATION

- The element of air or wind in Cherokee tradition is associated with the direction of the east and the season of spring. These connections offer us insights into the gifts air has to offer us. The east is the place of the rising sun, the breaking open of morning, and new beginnings after the long night of darkness and slumber. Dawn is the time of awakening and seeing the day ahead as full of possibility. Spring is a season of blossoming and burgeoning forth of the earth after the long winter's rest. It is a time to tend to the buds poking through the fertile soil and watch for the shape of the flowering to come. It is a time to celebrate abundance and newness.

- Take time each morning to begin the day with gratitude for the gifts of the Spirit. Allow the dawn to be a time of praying with air and honoring *ruach*, the holy breath that sustains you. Get in touch with your breathing. Give yourself time to tend to what is stirring in you those first few moments of the day, become aware of the blossoming that feels possible in this time of awakening. Inhale love, exhale fear.

- At the start of each day face the direction of the east, the direction of the dawn, and remember that Christ is imaged as the "bright morning star" (Rv 22:16). Close your eyes and breathe in the inspiration the Spirit offers to you. Create a space within you to receive whatever gifts this day will offer, unknown in this very moment. Rest in the anticipation and possibility of a new day. Ask yourself where you need a new beginning. Notice where in your body you experience the gifts of air and lightness.

- We all have places in our lives where we feel uninspired, where we are going through the motions. Pray with God's gift of air and imagine the Spirit blowing new life into those places where you have fallen asleep or have become deadened. Spend time asking for renewed vigor and energy, or try to notice if you are being invited to let those uninspired places go in order to make room for new possibilities.

- St. Ignatius of Loyola taught us the prayer of *Examen*, which essentially involves two main questions: When today did I experience my most life-giving moments? And when did I experience my most life-draining moments? Adapt this prayer and take time each morning to consider and, if possible, journal about where in your life (relationships, persons, experiences, places, dimensions of work or leisure) you receive the gift of inspiration and where you experience yourself having fallen asleep to life. Take note of any patterns over time.

- Allow your breath prayer to become a prayer of love and compassion. As you breathe in, receive God's gift of unending and expansive love for all of creation. As your breath expands your lungs, reflect on the ways in which love expands your heart. As you breathe out, "exhale" love to those for whom you care. Breathe out love to family and friends for five breaths. In the next five breaths expand your circle of awareness to include the people with whom you have challenging relationships. The next five breaths, expand again and breathe love onto your community. Keep expanding your circle of awareness to include all peoples, and finally all of the earth. Notice what is inspired in you when you practice extending love and care to the entire earth community.

- On a spring or summer day, go to the beach or the park and spend some time watching birds flying overhead. See if you can enter into their flight for a moment in your imagination. If you had wings, where would they carry you?

Carried by the Wind

The wind blows where it chooses, and you hear the
    sound of it,
but you do not know where it comes from or where
    it goes.
So it is with everyone who is born of the Spirit.

—John 3:8

A feather on the breath of God.

—Hildegard of Bingen

The Holy Spirit, the Paraclete—giver of everything
good—breathes where He wants and how He wants
and when He wants and keeps all secret inspiration
hidden.

—Gertrude the Great

Every moment and every event of every man's life
on earth plants something in his soul. For just as
the wind carries thousands of winged seeds, so each
moment brings with it germs of spiritual vitality that
come to rest imperceptibly in the minds and wills of
men and women. Most of these unnumbered seeds
perish and are lost, because men and women are not
prepared to receive them: for such seeds as these
cannot spring up anywhere except in the soil of
freedom, spontaneity and love.

—Thomas Merton

Peregrinatio is the Latin word for "pilgrimage." In Celtic tradition, peregrinatio takes on a special meaning as it refers to a different kind of pilgrimage. Instead of setting out to journey to a specific place, the ancient Celtic monks would undertake a journey to find their "place of resurrection," which is the place to which God is calling the wanderer to settle and await death. The best known example is St. Brendan, a sixth-century Celtic monk who left behind all that was safe and secure and, accompanied by twelve other monks, set out to sea. The boats used at the time were called coracles, which were small vessels made of animal skins stretched across a wooden frame and sealed with pitch. Brendan and others would set off in a coracle without oars, trusting the wind and current to guide them to arrive where they were being called to go. They would literally cast themselves adrift at sea for the love of God, following only the direction the wind would take them, happy to accept whatever the outcome might be.

These journeys were acts of complete trust and faith in the God who guides our journey and accompanies us along the way. To us, they serve as examples of surrender to the Spirit and a letting go of our own agendas. This kind of journey eventually became known as "white martyrdom," in contrast to the "red martyrdom" of the early Christian Church when believers sacrificed their lives for their beliefs. The white martyrs relinquished their sense of safety and ego to go where God called. In peregrinatio, the journey is initiated by an inner prompting, to leave behind the familiar and go where the Spirit leads. It means becoming a stranger to what is comfortable and secure, and an exile to what is safe. The story of Abraham in the Book of Genesis is the exemplar of leaving home in response to God's call, not knowing where the journey would lead.

While you may not want to cast yourself out to sea and leave your journey to the direction of the wind, you can pray with this gift of wind by considering the ways in your own life in which you are being invited to let go of some of your own goals and to begin to listen to the inner promptings of the Spirit. Praying with wind is an invitation to surrender to a less self-directed path through life in order to move toward a path that is more Spirit-directed. Wind beckons us to release our grip of control and enter into a life where we are willing to be led to new places.

FOR REFLECTION

- How might you lean into the Source that supports and buoys you and trust the direction it takes?

- Can you allow your sails to open fully, knowing that the wind blows where it wills?

- Are you able to release what is familiar and take steps to embrace the new?

- What would it mean for you to allow yourself to be carried through life as a feather, floating on the holy breath of the One who first breathed life into us?

PRAYING WITH WIND AS GUIDING FORCE

- The poet David Whyte, in his wonderful poem "What to Remember When Waking," writes that in the very first moment of morning after we awaken "there is a small opening into the new day / which closes the moment you begin your plans." He goes on to say: "What you can plan is too small for you to live." The central idea behind the Celtic journey of peregrinatio is to recognize the deep truth of this fact. Planning and goal-setting can be very helpful ways of getting things done, but because they are designed by our egos, these plans are too small for the life God calls us to. Often we forget to allow room for the Spirit in our planning. Invite into your prayer a freedom from planning and breathe into the possibilities God offers in each moment.

- Consider taking this adventure of peregrinatio in your imagination. Close your eyes and imagine you are setting yourself adrift in the sea of God's love or releasing yourself as a feather on God's breath. Allow yourself to let this journey unfold in your imagination for several minutes, and notice what stirs in you. Do you see any images or colors? Do you experience any new insights about the places calling for your release? Try this meditation sometime while lying on the grass on a summer day, observing the birds as they ride the currents of the air or clouds drifting, and see if they have any wisdom to offer to you.

- Begin each day by intentionally setting aside your plans and offering a prayer asking for direction from the flow of the Spirit present in the wind. Notice during the day where this guidance wants to take you.

- Hildegard of Bingen, the great twelfth-century Benedictine abbess, offers us the image of being "a feather on the breath of God." Take a moment to breathe into this image and imagine how you might live into this in your own life. The element of air invites us into a sense of trust and surrender to the invisible forces of our lives; it invites us to follow where the Spirit leads us.

- On your altar, place a feather and some incense to remind you of the qualities of air and wind.

God in the Whirlwind

From its chamber comes the whirlwind, and cold
from the scattering winds. . . .
Then the LORD answered Job out of the whirlwind:
"Who is this that darkens counsel by words without
knowledge? Gird up your loins like a man, I will
question you, and you shall declare to me. Where
were you when I laid the foundations of the earth?"

—Job 37:9, 38:1–4

On that day, when evening had come he said to
them, "Let us go across to the other side." And
leaving the crowd behind, they took him with them
in the boat, just as he was. Other boats were with

him. A great windstorm arose, and the waves beat
into the boat, so that the boat was already being
swamped. But he was in the stern, asleep on the
cushion; and they woke him up and said to him,
"Teacher, do you not care that we are perishing?" He
woke up and rebuked the wind and said to the sea,
"Peace! Be still!" Then the wind ceased and there was
dead calm. He said to them, "Why are you afraid?
Have you still no faith?" And they were filled with
great awe and said to one another, "Who then is this
that even the wind and the sea obey him?"

—Mark 4:35–41

Entering into the little boat he causes a storm to
arise upon the sea, and causes the wind to blow and
the waves to swell up. This storm arose not of its
own accord, but in obedience to his power, "who
brings forth winds out of his stores." He commands
the winds and the sea as their Lord, and upon a
sea tossed about and swollen by a great wind and a
great tempest, there comes a great calm. By these
happenings the Lord gave us a figure and image of
his teaching, that we might be patient in the face of
every storm.

—Origen

There are times in our lives when we feel as though we have
been caught in the midst of a great storm, buffeted about by life's
unexpected turns. Winds of change we did not anticipate may rise
so suddenly we have trouble regaining our foothold. Each of the elements offers us much beauty to contemplate, but they also offer us
an opportunity to meditate on the challenges of our lives and times

of suffering when the firm foundation we have come to rely upon is shaken and crumbling.

Storms are an inevitable and unavoidable part of life. Sometimes the most painful part of an experience of suffering or loss is that it causes us to question our understanding of who God is and how God works in the world. Our theological frameworks begin to unravel. When we are faced with a broken relationship, a lost dream, the loss of a job, or the death of someone dear to us, our hearts are broken open. The winds that come to blow us in a new direction are not always welcome.

The book of Job is a story that wrestles with the question of evil and suffering. It asks why a good man should have to suffer so much pain and what role God plays in that experience. In the very midst of the storm, God speaks directly to Job. There is a mutual conversation, Job cries out, and God responds "out of the whirlwind." God's response is not meant to be an easy or linear explanation but an invitation to humility and reverence before the awe of creation. In the face of our suffering, easy answers do not satisfy over the long range of life. What is important, the scriptures teach us, is to continue to wrestle with God and to bring our pain before our Creator. We are invited to remember that God is present right in the midst of our own grief. The point of Job is not to solve the problem of suffering but to illuminate how a person of integrity faces his or her own pain by continuing to engage God and by continuing to listen for the sacred presence in the midst of the whirlwind of life.

When my mother died quite suddenly several years ago, I was filled with grief and sorrow at her loss. I found myself angry at God for the whirlwind I was thrown into, not only of the pain of her loss, but also the whirl of the many practical details and tasks that death brings. I was blessed with a wise spiritual director who allowed me space for my grief and who encouraged me to express my anger at God freely. I slowly found comfort on my long morning walks. I rediscovered the God breathing through creation in those moments.

FOR REFLECTION

- Recall a time when you experienced deep suffering. What were the ways God continued to be present to you through that time? Was there a friend who listened well? A loyal companion animal who comforted you? A sacred place that offered you solace?

- When life becomes difficult, are you able to bring your own sorrow and pain to God in conversation? What keeps you from bringing the whole of yourself before God?

- Are you more apt to come to God in sorrow asking for relief rather than seeking to understand what lessons the experience might hold? How might you embrace the gifts hidden in suffering rather than trying to banish it?

PRAYING IN THE MIDST OF LIFE'S STORMS

- The psalms of lament are the ancient cries of our spiritual ancestors in the midst of their own pain. They offer us consolation that we are not alone in our suffering, and they offer us a template for our prayer, giving us permission to cry out to God.

- Consider praying with the words of Psalm 13:

  How long, LORD? Will you utterly forget me? How long will you hide your face from me?

  How long must I carry sorrow in my soul, grief in my heart day after day? How long will my enemy triumph over me?

  Look upon me, answer me, LORD, my God! Give light to my eyes lest I sleep in death,

  Lest my enemy say, "I have prevailed," lest my foes rejoice at my downfall.

  I trust in your faithfulness. Grant my heart joy in your help, That I may sing of the LORD, "How good our God has been to me!"

- Write your own psalm of lament. This is the general format:

1. Write your address to God, an invocation of God's name.

2. Write your complaint to God: a description of the problem, questions you want to ask God.

3. Affirmation of trust: this is the turning point of the psalm.

4. Petition: write your plea for God's intervention.

5. Write your acknowledgment of response and vow of praise and worship.

6. Close with a Doxology: blessings, praise.

Pray the words of your psalm aloud each morning as an honest cry of your soul to God.

- Express your feelings in words, using descriptive language to convey the depth and range of how you feel. Explore the whirlwind as closely as you can. Name what it is that you desire from God. Give yourself permission to speak from your heart. Demand to be heard by God by joining with the writer of Psalm 28: "Hear the sound of my pleading when I cry to you, lifting my hands toward your holy place."

- Sometimes in the midst of difficult times, the simplest prayer is the most effective. Take time each day to return to your breath and remember the Spirit that sustains you moment by moment. Breathing from deep in the belly relaxes our nervous system. When we are anxious we tend to breathe in a shallow way that reinforces our anxiety. Allow your breath to carry you through difficult moments.

- The story of Jesus calming the storm mirrors the first creation story and reminds us of God's power over the strong winds we experience. Take some quiet moments during your day and see if you can get in touch with the experience of the storm in your life. Imagine Jesus stepping in to provide a sense of calm. You might use a prayer of the imagination, based on the teachings of St. Ignatius of Loyola. He invites us to enter into the scripture story and experience the whole scene as if we were standing right there in its midst. Notice the colors, the quality of light and dark, the smells and sounds. Gaze lovingly at the disciples, taking in their whole appearance, and watch their expressions change as Jesus calms the storm. Notice your own bodily response to this experience. Breathe in their calm. Close this prayer with what Ignatius calls a *colloquy*, which is essentially a conversation with Jesus, about your experience of the storm and what it is you desire.

Lectio Divina with Wind

Lectio divina is an ancient contemplative prayer practice used to allow scripture to speak to our hearts and to help us to discover the multiple ways God dwells there. It means "sacred reading," and this practice can be extended beyond the reading of scripture to that other great book of revelation—nature. Lectio invites us to enter into silence and stillness to listen deeply for the stirring of the holy in the sacred texts around us. I recommend you try practicing lectio divina outdoors on a warm, dry day in order to listen more deeply to what the element of wind might reveal about God.

Preparation

Allow yourself twenty to thirty minutes of uninterrupted time. At the heart of lectio divina is cultivating the ability to listen deeply, to hear "with the ear of our hearts," as St. Benedict encourages us to do. When we read the scriptures we are invited to follow the example of the prophet Elijah, who listened for the still, small voice of God (I Kgs 19:12), the "faint murmuring sound" that is God's word for us and God's voice touching our hearts. This deep listening is a process of attuning ourselves to the presence of God. In order to hear this still, small voice, we must learn to love silence. Our modern culture surrounds us with noise from the television, radio, video games, constant conversation, and mental chatter. It takes some time to transition from the noise of our day to a place of deep stillness where we can listen deeply. Use whatever method is best for you, and allow yourself to enjoy silence for a few moments.

Sit or lie down comfortably, shifting your body so you feel relaxed and open. Take as much time as you need to turn inward and settle into stillness. It is often helpful to notice your breathing: with the in-breath, breathe in an awareness of the presence of the Spirit; with the out-breath, breathe out all that distracts you from this time of prayer.

Reading God's Word

Become aware of the way wind is present in the world around you—through a breeze blowing, through birds flying, butterflies fluttering, seeds being scattered by the wind, your own breath. In this initial encounter with the element of air, listen for one of its manifestations. Notice if the birds, the butterflies, the breeze, the seeds, your breath, or some other form invites you or stirs you. Listen for the way God might be calling you to deeper attention to wind this day. Listen until you have a sense of which manifestation of air is inviting you, and then spend some time savoring it.

Reflecting on God's Word

Continue to savor this aspect of air or wind, and then allow it to unfold in your memory and imagination and to work within you to speak even more deeply. Notice what feelings, memories, or images arise for you. Allow the Spirit to expand your capacity for listening and to open you to a fuller experience of the element at work in the world. Begin to notice where its qualities touch your life. What do you see, hear, touch, or remember? What is evoked in you? Allow it to interact with your thoughts, your hopes, your memories, your desires. Rest in this awareness for some time.

Responding to God's Word

After a time of resting in what the element evokes in you, you will be moved to deeper insight and a desire to respond and say yes to God. When this time comes, attend to the way the unfolding of the element connects with the context and situation of your life right now. How does it relate to what you have heard and seen this day? How does it connect with what is happening at home, at work, in your leisure time? Set aside a few minutes to explore this connection. How is God present to you there? Is God calling you to anything in your present circumstances? Is there a challenge presented here? Address your response to God in whatever way seems appropriate.

Resting with God's Word

Finally, simply rest in the presence of the One who has spoken to you intimately and personally. Rest in the silence of God's loving embrace, and allow your heart to be moved to gratitude for this time of prayer. Allow yourself to simply be in God's presence and breathe deeply of God's grace.

More Air and Wind Quotations for Prayer

These quotations are provided for a deepening of your prayer experience with the element of wind or air. Consider taking one quotation each morning to dwell with. Select a word or phrase to carry with you throughout the day and carry in your heart. You might also use the more traditional practice of lectio divina to pray with these words and discover how God is speaking to you through the text about the element.

The soul that has devoted itself to God journeys
along a rarely traveled path that soars.

—Mechtild of Magdeburg

Wisdom—omnipotent moving—
embracing this world,
informing everything that is

and everything that has life
in one unending circle.

You have three wings.
The first unfolds and flies through the highest sky.
The second dips down, touching the earth.
The third whirls its way over, under, and
through all things.

We praise You, Wisdom, for You are worthy of praise.

—Hildegard of Bingen

Love says, "The soul is like an eagle because the soul
     flies high,
yes, higher than any other bird, because she's
     feathered with fine love."

—Marguerite Porete

The soul rides on the feathers of the wind.

—Meister Eckhart

But soon there breathed a wind on me.
Nor sound nor motion made. Its path was not upon
     the sea, In ripple or in shade.
It raised my hair, it fanned my cheek, like a meadow-
     gale of spring
It mingled strangely with my fears. Yet it felt like a
     welcoming.
Swiftly, Swiftly flew the ship, Yet she sailed softly too:
Sweetly, sweetly blew the breeze—On me alone it
     blew . . .

—Samuel Taylor Coleridge

God's Soul is the wind rustling plants and leaves,
the dew dancing on the grass
the rainy breezes making everything grow.
Just like this, the kindness of a person flows, touching
those dragging burdens of longing.
We should be a breeze helping the homeless
dew comforting those who are depressed,
the cool, misty air refreshing the exhausted,
and with God's teaching we have got to feed the
hungry:

This is how we share God's soul.

—Hildegard of Bingen

Fold your wings, my soul,
Those wings you had spread wide
to soar to the terrestrial peaks
where the light is most ardent:
it is for you simply to wait
the descent of the fire—supposing it to be willing
to take possession of you.

—Pierre Teilhard de Chardin

Thus says God, the LORD, who created the heavens
and stretched them out, who spread out the earth and
what comes from it, who gives breath to the people
upon it and spirit to those who walk in it.

—Isaiah 42:5

Bless the Lord all you winds; sing praise to him and
highly exalt him forever.

—Daniel 3:65

Let my prayer come like incense before you;
the lifting up of my hands, like an evening sacrifice.

—Psalm 141:2

Awake, O north wind,
  And come, O south wind!
Blow upon my garden,
  Let its fragrance be wafted abroad.
Let my beloved come to his garden,
  And eat its choicest fruits.

—Song of Songs 4:16

"The world is still being created, and it is Christ who
is reaching His fulfillment in it." When I heard and
understood that saying, I looked around and saw, as
though in an ecstasy, that through all nature I was
immersed in God. God is everywhere. . . . Every
breath that passes through me, envelops me, or
captivates me, emanates, without any doubt, from
the heart of God; like a subtle and essential energy, it
transmits the pulsations of God's will.

—Teilhard de Chardin

Blessing of Wind

Spirit of Creation,
in the beginning you blew over the waters,
coaxing the earth up from the depths of the sea,
and inviting all creatures to rise up on their own wings.

Spirit of Renewing Life,
you breathed into me in my very first moment,

invigorate me with your gift of energy and newness.
Continue to breathe expansively in me,
inviting me to a vision for what is possible in my life.

Spirit of Restlessness,
stir me from my longing for comfort that so often stifles me,
help me to release from the places that keep me stuck,
and guide me in the direction you would have me go.

Spirit of the Great Winds,
help me to hear your voice in the midst of the whirlwind of my
    life.
Grant me the trust to hold on while I am being buffeted by life's
    storms.

Blessings of wind be upon me.
May my sails billow wide,
May I breathe deeply the gift of inspiration,
May I be carried to the place of my resurrection,
May I be fully free.

chapter two

Brother Fire

All praise be Yours, my God, through Brother Fire,
Through whom You brighten up the night.
How beautiful he is, how gay!
Full of power and strength.

—St. Francis of Assisi

Deep peace of the shining stars to you, which stay invisible till darkness falls
and discloses their pure and shining presence beaming down in compassion
on our turning world.

—Celtic Prayer

Fire and Creation

The world is charged with the grandeur of God,
It will flame out like shining from shook foil.

—Gerard Manley Hopkins

There an angel of the LORD appeared to him in a
flame of fire out of a bush;
he looked and the bush was blazing, yet it was not
consumed.

—Exodus 3:2

If the landscape reveals one certainty, it is that the
extravagant gesture is the very stuff of creation. After
the one extravagant gesture of creation in the first
place, the universe has continued to deal exclusively
in extravagances, flinging intricacies and colossi
down aeons of emptiness. . . . The whole show has
been on fire from the word go. I come down to the
water to cool my eyes. But everywhere I look I see
fire; that which isn't flint is tinder, and the whole
world sparks and flames.

—Annie Dillard

I will try, like them
To be my own silence:
And this is difficult. The whole
World is secretly on fire. The stones
Burn, even the stones
They burn me. How can a man be still or
Listen to all things burning? How can he dare
To sit with them when

All their silence
Is on fire?

                    —Thomas Merton

See and taste the Flowing
Godhead through your Being;
Feel the Holy Spirit
Moving and compelling
You within the Flowing
Fire and Light of God.

                    —Mechtild of Magdeburg

Where Life Begins

> *Not in tidal pools but in the thermal vents*
> *between Earth's shifting plates in the Ring of Fire . . .*

The urges of Earth
are there:
in the hot, hidden
down-under places

between worlds
where surface meets
surface and melts
in the Opening.

This, then, is
the cosmic kiss
where all that
is hard touches
its own Other,
transforms
enticingly,

consummates
and makes
the Never-before.

Where no sun gives light,
no micron escapes
the Divine Fire
from Within, surging
and frothing to come forth

and secret clay
crystals merge
and marry
in such wet heat
of Meeting.

This is where
Life Begins then:
neither here nor there,
but all ways Between.

—Alla Renée Bozarth

The element of fire is often associated with the direction of the south and the season of summer. The south is the place of the mid-day heat, the fullness of the noonday sun, and the radiant warmth of summertime. Summer is a time of fruitfulness and activity. The gentle hum of bees and crickets creates the backdrop to this season. Everything is alive and lush. One of my favorite parts of summer is the farmers' market that returns to our neighborhood. I love wandering among stalls overflowing with sweet berries, round peaches, glorious greens, and buckets of fresh flowers. There is the woman who churns her own ice cream and sells it in cones to cool down from summer's heat. There is a lovely liveliness as shoppers fill the parking lot-turned-gathering-place and live music plays. This group of city neighbors has come together for a brief time to celebrate the gifts of summer's abundance.

When I was growing up, summer was a time of play and wonder. No schoolwork to be concerned about, I would visit my grandparents in Massachusetts and go swimming in the pond by their house. On the Fourth of July we would watch the fireworks bursting across the night sky in sprays of brilliant color and light handheld sparklers. I remember drawing shapes and words into the darkness as they dazzled with their flare. Fireflies would arrive and glow, appearing and disappearing in the night. Sometimes we would go to the beach and sit around a bonfire, where I always had the sense that I was participating in something very primal, a ritual that has been going on for thousands of years. Our ancestors shared stories while gathered around the warmth of blazing flames, underneath the ink-blue darkness splattered with fiery stars.

The winters in the Pacific Northwest where I live are dark and wet. With fewer hours of daylight and long, rainy nights, our fireplace becomes a place of sanctuary in our home. The fire provides some warmth against the night chill, but even more than the warmth, the dancing flames provide a source of inspiration in the middle of winter. I can spend hours simply watching the fire burn, gazing at the flames as they rise and fall. Our home is spread with candle holders, and I love to illuminate them all on a winter evening and bask in their glow.

Each day as I sit down to write, I say a prayer to begin. While writing this chapter I have added to my prayer the lighting of a candle so that I might contemplate the element of which I am writing. I pray that I might be filled with the fire of passion and that I may share it with others through these words.

In this chapter you are invited to explore the impact of fire on your own prayer and spiritual life: the fire of illumination, of purification, the invitation to become fire, the living flame of love that burns within us, and to contemplate the fire in the sky of the sun, moon, and stars.

Getting in Touch with the Element of Fire

- Light a bonfire outdoors or a fire in your fireplace and gather your friends together to tell stories while experiencing the warmth of flame.
- Spread out a blanket under the night sky and watch the stars.
- Go into a church and light candles, offering prayers for those who need warmth.
- Go for a vigorous walk and notice the heat rising in your body.
- Find ways to support those in your community who cannot afford their winter heating bills.
- Feel the heat of the sun on your skin.
- Buy a bouquet of summertime sunflowers.

Fire of Illumination

As you well know, all the flame and glowing in heaven and on earth whichever burns and shines flows from God alone.

—Mechtild of Magdeburg

You who are the true light that is clearer than any light and deeper than any depth, chose to enlighten my darkness.

—St. Gertrude the Great

In the dead of night he suddenly beheld a flood of light shining down from above more brilliant than the sun, and . . . the whole world was gathered up before his eyes in what appeared to be a single ray of light.

—Pope St. Gregory the Great

You are the light of the world. . . let your light shine before others.

—Matthew 5:14–16

You are the sun
I am the dew
Gifted with life for a moment or two
That I for my time
May sparkle and shine
O Sun, come fill me with you
O Sun, come fill me with you.

—Peter Mayer

We sing the glories of this pillar of fire,
The brightness of which is not diminished,
Even when its light is divided and borrowed. . . .
May he who is the morning star find it burning—
That morning star which never sets,
That morning star which, rising again from the grave,
Faithfully sheds light on all the human race.

—The Exsultet (Easter Proclamation)

It is necessary for me to see the first point of light
which begins to be dawn. It is necessary to be present
alone at the resurrection of Day, in the solemn silence
at which the sun appears.

—Thomas Merton

Scripture is filled with images of light and fire as symbols of the ways in which God illuminates our world and our souls. Moses encounters God for the first time in a burning bush, and from those flames God speaks to Moses, telling him that God has heard the cry of his people and is calling upon Moses to help set the Israelites free. This vision of fire is also a call to freedom. After the escape from Egypt, God sent a pillar of fire to guide the Israelites across the desert by night as an ongoing beacon for guidance.

In the gospel story of the Transfiguration, it says that Jesus "shone like the sun and his clothes became dazzling white" (Mt 17:2). Fire and illumination again become a window onto the divine. The burning light that once appeared to Moses in the bush now radiates from Jesus himself. For Gregory Palamas (a fourteenth-century Orthodox monk), it was the disciples who changed at the transfiguration, not Christ. Christ was transfigured "not by the addition of something he was not, but by the manifestation to his disciples of what he really was. He opened their eyes so that instead of being blind they could see."

Because their perception grew sharper, they were able to behold Christ as he truly is, a source of radiance in the world. We will only see the light that already exists if we train ourselves to do so. To peer into a deeper reality is a metaphysical endeavor, requiring that we "see" with more than merely our eyes, and that we sense with more than merely our natural senses. The discipline of spiritual practice helps us to cultivate our ability to see below the surface of things, to have a transfigured vision of the world.

According to legend, in the time of St. Patrick a fire was kindled each spring by Celtic tribes, and one year Patrick decided to dedicate this fire to the risen Christ. This is said to be the origin of the fire lit on the Easter vigil. Each year on this sacred night we stand outside and light the great fire outdoors and process with it into the sanctuary where the Easter candle is lit as a reminder of the light God brings to the world. Then we pass that light to one another, each person holding a taper illumined by the flame rising from it. We light candles in our own prayer space, signaling the presence of a great fire burning among us. We are each illumined by the fire lit within us, shining out to the world.

Sometimes for prayer, I engage in a "walking" lectio divina, choosing a text and praying with it as I walk. Recently, the passage above about an experience St. Benedict had at the end of his life had my heart burning: "The whole world was gathered up before his eyes / in what appeared to be a single ray of light." I took these words on a walk with me, entering with Benedict into his final vision. I began by relishing the words themselves, savoring them within me. Then I allowed my imagination to unfold, to let images, feelings, and memories stir in me. I was flooded with images of creation infused with radiant light—sitting by the sea, walking deep in the woods, climbing a mountain, breathing in a field of wildflowers—each place luminous and connected in a sacred way to the others through this luminosity.

From these images and memories rising up in me, I listened for the invitation God had for me. How am I being called in response to what I have seen and heard in my prayer? It was springtime and I turned a corner and saw clusters of daffodils splayed across patches of grass. White and gold petals were open in their own prayers of supplication, illuminated by sunlight. In a moment of grace, I saw the daffodil was not radiant just because of the sunlight dancing across its surface. Suddenly the daffodil was lit from within. The sun merely calls this spark of God forth, the spark residing within each person and each extravagant moment of creation.

I saw that as it is with the daffodil, so it is with me as well. The sunlight spread across my skin, warming me with its radiant heat. And in this way, the sun reminded me of the way God illuminates me from within, dwells deep within me as a spark. When I open my heart I become a burning flame. My invitation is to carry this light into the world and to see fire everywhere I look.

FOR REFLECTION

- What radiance awaits you today if you only take time to look and really see?

- What is the invitation of fire for you this day?

- What is blazing in your heart?

- Where in your life do you experience the fire of light, protection, and warmth?

- How might you receive the inspiration of fire burning through all of creation?

PRAYING WITH THE ILLUMINATING GIFTS OF FIRE

- In Cherokee tradition, fire is associated with the season of summer and the middle of the day. At noontime, the point when the light of the day grows strongest, pause for a moment from whatever you are doing and honor the fire of the day. Face south and say a prayer asking to receive the gift of illumination in the midst of your daily life.

- Place a candle on your altar. Light it each day as you begin your time of prayer, and take a moment to honor the gift of light and the warmth of fire. Offer gratitude for the gifts of courage and passion that fire brings to your life.

- Read this prayer from Hildegard of Bingen aloud slowly, imagining yourself participating in this fiery power:

  I, the highest and fiery power, have kindled every spark of life . . . I, the fiery life of divine essence, am aflame beyond the beauty of the meadows, I gleam in the waters, and I burn in the sun, moon, and stars. With every breeze, as with invisible life that contains everything, I awaken everything to life. The air lives by turning green and being in bloom. The waters flow as if they were alive. The sun lives in its light, and the moon is enkindled, after its disappearance, once again by the light of the sun so that the moon is again revived. . . . And thus I remain hidden in every kind of reality as a fiery power. Everything burns because of me in the way our breath constantly moves us, like the wind-tossed flame in a fire.

- Sigurd F. Olson said,

  I know now as men accept the time clock of the wilderness, their lives become entirely different. It is one of the great compensations of primitive experience, and when one finally reaches the point where days are governed by daylight and dark, rather than by schedules, where one eats if hungry and sleeps when tired, and becomes completely immersed in the ancient rhythms, then one begins to live.

- Take a retreat when you can allow yourself to be "governed by daylight and dark," resting when the sun goes down rather than continuing to push forward, and rising when the sun does, greeting the new day. What do you discover when you allow yourself to live into these "ancient rhythms"? What do you notice about the world's rising and falling and your own?

- Imagine the fire burning within you and within every living thing. Go for a walk on a sunny day and see if you can transform your vision of the world, discovering the fire burning in each person you pass, in each tree and flower and animal. Then see if you can discover this fire within yourself.

- Take time to watch the sunrise or sunset and breathe in the beauty of the fiery sky. Contemplate what those beginnings and endings have to say to your own life.

Fire of Purification

You, God, are a fire that always burns without consuming. You are a fire consuming in its heat every compartment of the soul's self-absorbed love. You are a fire lifting all chill and giving all light. In Your light You show me Your truth. You're the Light that outshines every Light.

You, God, give the mind's eye Your divine light so
completely and excellently, You bring lucidity even
to the light of faith. In that faith, I see my soul has
life, and in that light, I receive You who are Light
itself.

—St. Catherine of Siena

See, I have refined you, but not like silver;
I have tested you in the furnace of adversity.

—Isaiah 48:10

The crucible is for silver, and the furnace is for gold,
but the Lord tests the heart.

—Proverbs 17:3

One late night in Seattle, where I live in a dense urban neighborhood, there were sirens wailing and lights flashing outside of our
apartment window. My husband and I arose to look outside, and we
were shocked to see the apartment building on the opposite corner
from ours engulfed in flames. As I was mesmerized by the force of
the fire, I whispered prayers that the people who lived in the homes
would be safely rescued.

While fire is a source of life and warmth, it can also be a profoundly destructive element. In recent years we have seen on the
news wildfires rage in California and Australia. Sometimes these are
ignited by human interference, sometimes by nature herself through
lightning strikes, volcanic discharges, or the hot, dry conditions
that occur when rain hasn't fallen in some time. While the fire can
spread out of control and destroy homes and communities, often
the fire also has a renewing effect on the landscape. I remember several years ago driving up to the coast in Northern California, where
the area had been affected by wildfires a couple of years prior. I was
saddened to see the charred stumps of trees where lush forest once

stood. And yet I also saw hundreds of tiny fresh young saplings just beginning to sprout and renew the land. I beheld this paradox of destruction and renewal and felt profoundly hopeful in the midst of my sadness. I could see the cycle of death and new life here.

We experience this paradoxical effect of fire in our own lives. There are times when it may feel like a fire has raged through our lives, destroying all that we have held dear. Times of suffering also remind us of what is most vital in our lives. The passages from Isaiah and Proverbs above point to this understanding of God's fire as a process of purification and refinement. We often call this experience of purgation a "desert experience" because of the desert's heat and harsh conditions. The desert's conditions, with too little water and too much sun, are just barely supportive of life. But life does indeed survive and even flourish within the confines of its harsh restrictions. The desert is also the place where we can face our own demons and shadows and be cleansed of them. After Jesus' baptism, he went to the desert for forty days to prepare himself for his ministry by confronting Satan and his temptations. We are similarly invited into the desert of the soul for Lent in reflection of Jesus' journey and in order to search for our own refinement and transformation.

On Palm Sunday we raise our palm branches to herald the arrival of Jesus into Jerusalem to begin his final earthly journey. Those palms are then burned, and the ashes are used for Ash Wednesday service the following year at the beginning of Lent. We are marked by those ashes to start the season of purification, of letting go, as a reminder of our mortality and what is most essential in our lives. The purgative gift of fire is expressed starkly in a haiku by Japanese poet Masahide, who writes:

> Barn's burnt down—
> Now
> I can see the moon.

Grief is one of those desert places where our hearts are broken wide open and tears flow across the parched places in our souls. I have held the ashes of loved ones in my hands. I have been startled to see their once vibrant and alive bodies reduced to a pile of dust. I never imagined in those times of profound sorrow that I would come to a place of new life. The desert journey through fire for me was a very long one. However, when it comes to the fire of purification, there really is no way out but through.

FOR REFLECTION

- What in your life needs to be refined or purified?
- What have been the desert experiences of your life?
- Where has God offered renewal and rebirth?
- Where do you experience resistance to the purifying dimensions of fire?

PRAYING WITH THE PURIFYING GIFTS OF FIRE

- Keep a small bowl of ashes or sand on your altar space to remind you of the desert places of your life.

- Take some time each season to write down on small strips of paper the things in your life you want to let go of. Lay them in a metal bowl outdoors with a source of water nearby, and burn them. As you watch the flames purifying your prayers, ask for the strength to truly surrender those things which have a hold on your life. Consider gathering with a small group to share these together.

- Reflect on the places in your life where you still carry grief for losses you have not yet fully mourned. We all have them. Our culture discourages us from really tending to our sorrow and encourages us to "move on." Where has there been an invitation into the desert of purification that you have pushed aside because of its discomfort? Can you contemplate going there now, accompanied by the support of friends and a spiritual director?

Becoming Fire

Abba Lot came to Abba Joseph and said:

Father, according as I am able, I keep my little
rule, and my little fast, my prayer, meditation, and
contemplative silence; and, according as I am able,
I strive to cleanse my heart of thoughts: now what
more should I do?

The elder rose up in reply and stretched out his
hands to heaven, and his fingers became like ten
lamps of fire.

He said: Why not become fire?

—Desert Fathers

Lie down in the fire and see and taste the flowing
Godhead in your being. Feel the Holy Spirit move in
you, compelling you to love God, His fire, and His
flowing in many different ways.

—Mechtild of Magdeburg

Overwhelmed by love, I said, "Lord, how I want my soul
to burn with such fire that it would melt and become
liquid so it could be poured—all of it—into You!"

God answered, "Your will is such a fire for you."

—St. Gertrude the Great

Go, set the world on fire.

—St. Ignatius of Loyola

I love the story from the desert fathers above. In the spiritual life we keep our practices, spend time in prayer, seek God in all things, and yet at some point even all this is not enough—and we are asked to become fire. Becoming fire means letting our passion for life and beauty ignite us in the world. It means, as St. Ignatius of Loyola wisely said, that we are called to set the whole world on fire with our passion for God.

We may find ourselves drawn to creative expression because it taps into what is most vital and alive in us. This burning in our blood seeks expression in the world, whether through art, song, cooking, gardening, our work, relationships, or in our presence to others. Becoming fire means saying yes to life by the very way we live.

St. Ignatius of Loyola spoke of the deepest desires of our hearts as planted there by God. Often we have been taught to mistrust our desires, to hold them with suspicion. Through the Spiritual Exercises, Ignatius developed a retreat that incorporates a set of tools for distinguishing our truest, deepest desires as those that God wants passionately for us. The Exercises invite us into a process of listening for what we desire in order to discern which desires come from our own egos and wills and which come from God. When we are in touch with our deepest, God-given desires, we can allow ourselves to become united with the fire that dwells within us.

In recent years we have heard the term "fire in the belly" be claimed for the men's spirituality movement. It was the title of a book, by philosopher Sam Keen, inviting men to reclaim the vitality and passion found within. The original source of this metaphor is unknown but perhaps derives from the stoking of a pot-bellied stove. Do you have a fire in your belly, or has it become dampened by life's demands? Whether male or female, we are each invited to kindle our passion for life and God. Fire symbolizes what we are most passionate about, what we love most, where we stoke the flames of courage. It is the source of our vitality and energy.

In the second chapter of Acts of the Apostles, we read that at Pentecost there appeared to the disciples "tongues as of fire, which parted and came to rest on each one of them." The apostles had been gathered together in the upper room, uncertain of what to do next.

Pentecost is a story of the fire of courage being breathed into those earliest followers.

FOR REFLECTION

- What is the invitation of fire for you this day?
- What is blazing in your heart?
- Where do you need the fire of courage in your life?
- What keeps you from living your life with an awareness of this holy fire within you?
- What ignites you with sacred passion for the world?
- What would it mean for you to truly become fire?

PRAYING TO BECOME FIRE

- Our internal fire maintains our body heat and keeps us alive. Take some time in prayer to get in touch with your body's fire through your pulse and the beating of your heart. Rest your hand on your heart and find your heartbeat. Feel the warmth of your body rising up from your skin and give thanks for the gift of being alive. Go for a long walk, and pause every so often to experience the rising heat in your body and to feel your body's pulse speeding up.

- On the feast of Pentecost wear the color red. This feast is often called the "birthday of the Church." Consider making this feast the birthday of your own courage being infused into your life and summoning you out into the world.

- Each day write down where you experience your desire leading you. What are the longings of your heart that go unfulfilled? What are the activities of your life that kindle the fire within you? How do you live in alignment with God's call and become fire? Remember: fire isn't orderly; it doesn't take prescribed patterns but blazes where it will. What are the desires that don't seem to rise from God, that seem to take your energy away or feel compulsive?

- Sometimes our inner fires seem to die, to fizzle out. At these times we are often overworked, overcommitted, or undernourished with the things that bring our souls alive. At the end of each day take a few moments to notice what kindled your heart during the day. Reflect on what made your soul feel alive, and offer a prayer for courage to live into what sets you on fire. Journal about this over several days, and see if you begin to notice a pattern.

Living Flame of Love

O living flame of love . . .
O lamps of fire
in whose splendors
the deep caverns of feeling,
once obscure and blind,
now give forth, so rarely, so exquisitely,
both warmth and light to their Beloved.

How gently and lovingly
you wake in my heart,
where in secret you dwell alone;
and in your sweet breathing,
filled with good and glory,
how tenderly you swell my heart with love.

—St. John of the Cross

The day will come when after we have mastered
the winds, the waves, the tides and gravity, we shall
harness for God the energies of love. Then for the
second time in the history of the world, [humankind]
will have discovered fire.

—Pierre Teilhard de Chardin

But the Lord, with great love, shows her the Divine
Heart. This heart glows like red gold in a great fire.
God lays the soul bare in his glowing heart.

—Mechtild of Magdeburg

Were not our hearts burning within us while he was
talking to us on the road, while he was opening the
scriptures to us?

—Luke 24:32

Many of the mystics, including John of the Cross, talk about
God as the living flame within each of us. We each contain a spark of
the divine, a holy fire that leads us to greater love. As the fourteenth-
century German mystic Meister Eckhart said, God is the spark of the
soul. I am often asked in spiritual direction or while leading retreats,
"How does a person know when he or she is having an authentic experience of God?" My response is simple: true prayer increases our
capacity for love, so that the circle of who is included in our love is
widened and the depth of our love is made more profound.

Several years ago I went on a contemplative retreat. It was the
height of summer, and each day the sun radiated and warmed us
during our quiet time for reflection. After the first presentation we
were asked to take some time, an hour or so, and be out in creation
and contemplate the love that God has for each part of creation. I
remember finding a spot on the cool grass in front of a grand oak
tree. Its graceful branches stretched upward toward the sky, its green
leaves shimmered in the afternoon breeze, its roots extended deep
into the moist earth. I experienced God's presence there. I knew for
a few brief moments the profound love God had for the tree's beauty, for its gift of oxygen to the world, for its witness to the beauty of
creation. I dwelled there in the fire of love, and I saw the living flame
burning in that tree and in all of creation.

We returned from this encounter to a second invitation. This time we were to imagine that same love we experienced for creation poured out onto ourselves. We were to see if we could receive the same love for ourselves, if we could meet God's loving gaze and experience the kindling of our own hearts. I returned to my spot on the grass, under the protective shade of the tree. It was very moving to shift this vision of the fire in all things to myself. Now, years later, I am still able to dwell there in this sense of profound love, and I find myself returning in my imagination to this experience again and again. Discovering this profound love for myself and for all of creation is a path toward unleashing the tremendous power of love into the world and, as Pierre Teilhard de Chardin says so poetically, discovering fire for the second time.

FOR REFLECTION

- When do you experience the inner flame of love burning most brightly within you?

- What practices help to kindle your passion to overflowing?

- What form does your inner fire take? What do you do to keep it fueled?

PRAYING TO KINDLE THE LIVING FLAME OF LOVE

- Spend some time outdoors basking in the love that God holds for all of creation. Once you are really in touch with the experience of God's fire burning in everything you see, shift your focus to yourself and see if you can hold the same vision for your own heart and being.

- Sit with your eyes closed and your hand on your heart. As you get in touch with the beating of your own heart, imagine the divine flame burning within you. Begin to send the fire of love outward, opening your heart as widely as you can. Spend some time pouring love onto your friends and family members, then extend the love to your community, then out to all of creation.

- Take time to light a fire in your fireplace or to light several candles, and simply rest in the presence of the flames. Gaze on them and see what they have to teach you about God who is the spark of your soul.

- Use the Ignatian prayer of the imagination to pray with the Emmaus story (Lk 24:13–35). Read it through once, and then close your eyes and imagine yourself there in the scene, walking alongside the disciples. Experience the unfolding of the story with all of your senses—notice the sights as you travel down the road, what you smell in the air around you; listen for the sounds of conversation and creatures around you; taste the bread that Jesus breaks; and feel the experience of having your heart burn in recognition of his presence there with you. Reflect on the places in your life where your heart had been burning but you did not take notice.

Sun, Moon, and Stars

I, the fiery life of divine essence, am aflame beyond
the beauty of the meadows, I gleam in the waters,
and I burn in the sun, moon, and stars.

—Hildegard of Bingen

O Splendor of the Father's Light
That makes our daylight lucid, bright;
O Light of light and sun of day,
Now shine on us your brightest ray.

True Sun, break out on earth and shine
In radiance with your light divine;
By dazzling of your Spirit's might,
Oh, give our jaded senses light.

—St. Ambrose of Milan

When they had heard the king, they set out; and
there, ahead of them, went the star that they had

seen at its rising, until it stopped over the place where the child was. When they saw that the star had stopped, they were overwhelmed with joy. On entering the house, they saw the child with Mary his mother; and they knelt down and paid him homage. Then, opening their treasure chests, they offered him gifts of gold, frankincense, and myrrh.

—Matthew 2:9–12

Not only were there more quasars in the ancient universe, but they were also more luminous. We can envy the brilliance of those early skies. The galaxies were closer together than they are now, and they burned with the light of many hot blue stars. At the centers of those great wheels of light, streams of matter plunged into black holes, pulled by gravity into knots of incredible density and permanent blackness—stars, planets, moons, rain and wind all absconded, gone. As the matter fell, it gave off energy that caused the galactic nuclei to glow with a light greater than that of all the stars in the heavens. The universe blazed with those luminous beacons. It was a time of light.

—Chet Raymo

There will be signs in the sun, the moon, and the stars.

—Luke 21:25

Most of us live in urban areas where the constant stream of light from artificial sources obscures our vision of the night sky. When I have the chance to get away from the city, I often enjoy looking at the black upturned bowl of the sky at night. Gazing up at the shimmering lights, I know that they are all stars like our sun, some of even greater magnitude, radiating such immense energy across the galaxy and beyond. These thousand tiny glittering points evoke awe in a God who is vast beyond our imaginings. The fire of the big bang still radiates across space and time. The Earth's core contains this fire, the universe is illuminated by it, and our bodies contain this heat within them. There is an amazement that comes when I recall that our planet has the perfect balance of light and atmosphere to create life. We are just the right distance from the sun to sustain the thriving of plants and animals of an enormous diversity.

The stars in the night sky were once an important navigational tool. In scripture we read about the wise men who followed the star to where Jesus lay and how Abraham was told by God that his descendants would number the stars (Gn 15:5). We might imagine how vast the night sky seemed to ancient peoples and how this promise from God was rooted in a sense of the immensity of the number of celestial bodies. As we take time to reconnect with the heavens, we can reconnect to this sense of awe that filled the hearts of our ancestors.

In his book *Drawing Closer to Nature*, Peter London writes:

> We too are remnants of that First Fire that ever since lights the heavens as well as the tiny fires that warm our brief lives. Our planet remembers this original heat deep within its core, as we do in our fashion. . . . The setting of our life's journey takes places upon a stage in which we spend half our allotted time in yellow light from a ball of Fire, the other half in pale blue light from a mirror-ball. We are diurnal creatures formed with all the rest of the biota upon a diurnal planet. The two lights provide us with different-appearing worlds, which in turn form our two different minds; the one that reasons and the one that dreams.

The sun and the moon shape our imaginations as they each illuminate our days and nights to varying degrees. The solar calendar is based upon the Earth's orbit around the sun of just over 365 days and invites us to a deeper awareness of the seasons and the changing nature of light, especially for those of us who live further from the equator. Winters where I live offer short, dark days, often with cloud cover muting the sun that remains low in the sky. Summer days are long with only a few hours of darkness for deep sleep. Sunrise and sunset stretch far apart from each other to offer up abundant light.

The lunar calendar is based on the moon's orbit around the earth of just over twenty-eight days. Both Jewish and Muslim traditions use the cycles of the moon to navigate feast days. The moon's waxing and waning offers a mirror of the sun's own rise and fall each day.

FOR REFLECTION

- When I contemplate the immensity of the universe, what is my experience?

- Can I imagine myself as a shining star or brilliant sun? What are the gifts I have to offer when I take on this form?

- How do the cycles of the sun and moon shape my own awareness and practice?

PRAYING WITH THE SUN, MOON, AND STARS

- While fire is the element associated with noontime, it is also the element that invites us to become aware of the different qualities of light throughout the day. Honor the sun at morning and evening as well as midday. Notice the different qualities of light present at each of these transition points. What does the fire found in the rising and setting of the sun have to say to your life?

- Keep track of the lunar cycles, making note of the full and new moons so you become aware of the rhythms of waxing and waning in the night sky.

- On a warm night go to a place where the reflective light is minimal and lie down under the stars, taking in the fire of the heavens. Practice a modified version of lectio divina with the night sky. Begin by stilling your mind and shift your seeing to the eyes of your heart (Eph 1:18). Scan the sky for a while, taking in the expansiveness of its beauty. Allow your eyes to slowly settle on a constellation or point of light that is drawing your attention. Savor this for a few moments, and then allow this light to kindle memories, feelings, and other images within you. Stay with these for several minutes. Receive the gift of God's invitation speaking to you through these. Where are you being invited to bring your fire? Allow your heart to receive this call. Spend some time in silence, simply resting in God's embrace. Complete this time of prayer by gazing again at the whole of the sky and seeing what you notice.

- Learn the names of some of the constellations, and see if you can identify them.

- Purchase or borrow a telescope, and bring the moon and stars near. Even a set of good binoculars can give you a heightened appreciation for the moon's surface.

- As we lie on our backs to stargaze, we naturally assume we are looking "up" at the sky. However, there is no up and down. When we stand up, we are really sticking out into space. Try lying on your back and imagining that you are looking down into the great black night. Practicing this perspective helps us to have an experience of the universe that is not so human-centered, but for a moment invites us into a "galactic perspective" (Uhl, *Developing Ecological Consciousness*, p. 13).

Lectio Divina with Fire

Preparation

Find a place where you can contemplate fire, perhaps in a quiet room with a candle burning or fireplace blazing. Sit comfortably, shifting your body so you feel relaxed and open. Take as much time as you need to turn inward and settle into stillness. With the in-breath, breathe in an awareness of the fiery presence of the Spirit;

with the out-breath, breathe out all that distracts you from this time of prayer.

Reading God's Word

Become aware of the flame dancing before you. Notice the aspect of fire that invites you or stirs you, whether the quality of light or the intensity of heat or the change of color. Listen for the way God might be calling you to deeper attention to fire this day. Listen until you have a sense of which manifestation of fire is inviting you, and then spend some time savoring it.

Reflecting on God's Word

Continue to savor this aspect of fire, and then allow it to unfold in your memory and imagination, and work within you to speak even more deeply. Notice what feelings, memories, or images arise for you. Allow the Spirit to expand your capacity for listening and to open you to a fuller experience of the element at work in the world. Begin to notice where its qualities touch your life. What do you see, hear, touch, or remember? What is evoked in you? Allow it to interact with your thoughts, your hopes, your memories, your desires. Rest in this awareness for some time.

Responding to God's Word

After a time of resting in what the element evokes in you, you will be moved to deeper insight and a desire to respond and say yes to God. When this time comes, attend to the way the unfolding of the element connects with the context and situation of your life right now. How does it relate to what you have heard and seen this day? How does it connect with what is happening at home, at work, in your leisure time? Take an extended time of exploring this connection. How is God present to you there? Is God calling you to anything in your present circumstances? Is there a challenge presented here? Address your response to God in whatever way seems appropriate.

Resting with God's Word

Finally, simply rest in the presence of the One who has spoken to you intimately and personally. Rest in the silence of God's loving embrace, and allow your heart to be moved to gratitude for this time of prayer. Anyone who has ever been in love knows that there are moments when no words are necessary, moments beyond words where you simply rest in the presence of your beloved. Allow yourself to simply be in God's presence. Rest in the fire of love as long as you need to.

More Fire Quotations for Prayer

I'm the secret fire in everything, and everything
    smells like Me.
The living breathe My sweet perfume,
    and they breathe out praise of Me.
They never die
    because I am their Life.

I flame out—intense, godly Life—over the shining
    fields of corn,
I glow in the shimmer of the fire's embers,
I burn in the sun and the moon and the stars.
The secret Life of Me breathes in the wind
    and holds all things together soulfully.

This is God's voice.

—Hildegard of Bingen

He spread out a cloud for a covering
and a fire to give light by night.

—Psalm 105:39

It is you who light my lamp; the Lord, my God, lights up my darkness.

—Psalm 18:28

The voice of the Lord flashes forth flames of fire.

—Psalm 29:7

I am the light of the world. Whoever follows me will never walk in darkness, but will have the light of life.

—John 8:12

Then there appeared to them tongues as of fire, which parted and came to rest on each one of them. And they were all filled with the holy Spirit and began to speak in different tongues, as the Spirit enabled them to proclaim.

—Acts 2:3–4

I have come to bring fire to the earth and how I wish it were already blazing.

—Luke 12:49

I return from the same walk a day later scarcely knowing my name. Litanies hum in my ears . . . alleluia! I cannot cause the light; the most I can do is try to put myself in the path of its beam. It is possible, in deep space, to sail on a solar wind. Light, be it particle or wave, has force: you rig a giant sail and go.

—Annie Dillard

Sunrise: hidden by pines and cedars to the east I saw
the red flames of the kingly sun glaring through the
black trees, not like dawn, but like a forest fire.

—Thomas Merton

One moment there had been nothing but darkness;
next moment a thousand, thousand points of light
leaped out—single stars, constellations, and planets,
brighter and bigger than any world. There were no
clouds. The new stars and the new voices began at
exactly the same time. If you had seen and heard it
. . . you would have felt quite certain that it was the
stars themselves which were singing, and that it was
the First Voice, the deep one, which had made them
appear and made them sing.

—C. S. Lewis

Blessing of Fire

Spirit of Fire,
You revealed yourself through the burning bush
And the fiery courage of Pentecost.

Fiery Spirit, Source of all creative power,
Kindle your Holy Spark within me,
Breathe into me your Sacred Passion,
Fill me with your Flame until I have become fire,
Offering warmth and light to the world.

Spirit of Refining Fire,
Help me to release what no longer serves me
To make room for your light to fill me.

Blessings of fire be upon me
May the light of God illuminate me

and may the flame of love burn brightly in me
May I discover each day anew my own hidden fire and
  enter it fully.

chapter three

Sister Water

All praise be Yours, my God, through Sister Water,
So useful, humble, precious, and pure.

—St. Francis of Assisi

Deep peace of the running wave to you, of water flowing,
rising and falling,
sometimes advancing, sometimes receding . . .

May the stream of your life flow unimpeded!
Deep peace of the running wave to you!

—Celtic Prayer

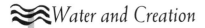

≈ *Water and Creation*

The Way God Approaches the Soul:
I come to my beloved as the dew on the flower.

—Mechtild of Magdeburg

Love, open on me—for I am very tiny—the viscera
of Your love and kindness. Open on me the cataracts
of Your gracious fatherly nurturing. Break over me
fountains of unlimited mercy. Absorb me in the
depths of Your love. Drown me in the flood of Your
living love, like a drop loses itself in the ocean's
fullness. Let me die in the tsunami of your immense
compassion, as a little spark of fire fizzles in the
stream's surging current. Let the raindrops of Your
kind love make me cling to You.

—St. Gertrude the Great

When the waters saw you, O God, when the waters
    saw you, they were afraid; the very deep trembled.
The clouds poured out water; the skies thundered;
    your arrows flashed on every side.
The crash of your thunder was in the whirlwind; your
    lightnings lit up the world; the earth trembled and
    shook.
Your way was through the sea, your path, through the
    mighty waters; yet your footprints were unseen.

—Psalm 77:16–19

God is a bright ocean that distills and reveals hidden
truths so that my soul has a better understanding of
how to trust Love, and this water is a mirror in which
You, Eternal Trinity, give me knowledge.

—Catherine of Siena

God is a river, not just a stone
God is a wild, raging rapids
And a slow, meandering flow
God is a deep and narrow passage
And a peaceful, sandy shoal
God is the river, swimmer
So let go.

—Peter Mayer

Say you are in the country; in some land of lakes.
Take almost any path you please, and ten to one it
carries you down in a dale, and leaves you there by
a pool in the stream. There is magic in it. . . . Yes, as
everyone knows, meditation and water are wedded
forever.

—Herman Melville

The element of water is often associated with the direction of
the west and the season of autumn. The west is the place of the setting sun, the ending of the day, and the transition into a time of
darkness. It is a time to recognize our own limitations and frailty.
Autumn is a season of letting go of what no longer serves us in preparation for the fallow time of winter. Dusk is a threshold time, a time
of transitions. The rising and falling of the tides connects us to the
movement and transition space of evening.

Human life itself begins in a watery womb. We spend our first
nine months of life in water and then emerge from this warm, dark

brine into the world. The waters break open when birth is impending. In the first creation story in Genesis, the waters existed before the light and the rest of creation emerged from the water. Water is essential to life. It pulses through our veins, making up 70 percent of the Earth's surface and 60 percent of our bodies. The beating of our blood echoes the rise and fall of our breathing, the great rhythms of the tides and the ebbing and flowing of the sea's great daily cycles that reflect the moon's phases.

We encounter water in many different forms—ocean, lake, fountain, river, rain, pool, puddle, tears. Water is malleable, appearing in different forms—steam, liquid, and ice. For ancient peoples, the sea was a place of great mystery and unending horizons. Psalm 104 proclaims: "Look at the sea, great and wide. It teems with countless beings, living things both large and small."

Water is also a dominant symbol in religious practice. Ritual bathing and hand washing for purification have a place in many traditions. In Christianity, the font of holy water is the place of baptism and initiation into the community. The priest washes his hands as the eucharistic prayer begins and drops a splash of water to mingle with the wine. In Jewish tradition, the *mikvah* is the holy bath, the place of purification and renewal. On Sabbath night a bowl and pitcher of water is passed around the table as a part of the prayer, so that the participants can wash themselves clean as a way of entering into this sacred time.

Here in the Northwest we live in a rainforest. Winters offer a constant mist of water, keeping the landscape lush and green. There is something beautiful to me about walking in the rain. It creates a kind of silence through its steady rhythm. Most of the time the rain is light, but at times it comes down hard, beating against my windows, and the sound is hypnotic. Growing up on the East Coast I used to love to listen to the thunderstorms of summertime, when water would rush from the sky in torrents, washing the world clean again. In those moments after a great storm, the air is charged and feels new and alive.

As I wrote and prepared this chapter on water, I added to my daily morning prayer a new ritual. Each day, I would dip my fingers in a small bowl and touch my forehead with it, praying that my spirit might be filled with the fluidity of water about which I write and that I may share it with others through my words.

In this chapter you are invited to explore the impact of water on your own prayer and spiritual life: the rise and fall of the tides, living water, wells, springs, fountains, the greening power of God, and baptism and blessing.

Getting in Touch with the Element of Water

- Walk in the rain.
- Sit and watch a park fountain or bird bath.
- Go swimming or sailing.
- Run through a sprinkler on a hot summer day with children.
- Give thanks for the gift of water, and support those who have limited access through a nonprofit such as Water Partners International (www.water.org).

Rise and Fall of the Tides

Leave me alone with God
as much as may be.
As the tide draws the waters close in upon the shore,
Make me an island, set apart,
alone with you, God, holy to you.

Then with the turning of the tide
prepare me to carry your presence to the busy world
        beyond,
the world that rushes in on me
till the waters come again and fold me back to you.

—St. Aidan of Lindisfarne

May what I do flow from me like a river,
no forcing and no holding back,
the way it is with children.
Then in these swelling and ebbing currents,
these deepening tides moving out, returning,
I will sing you as no one ever has, streaming through
    widening channels
into the open sea.

—Rainer Maria Rilke

No matter what your work, let it be your own.
No matter what your occupation, let what you are
    doing be organic.
Let it be in your bones.
In this way, you will open the door by which the
    affluence of heaven and earth shall stream into you.

—Ralph Waldo Emerson

Like the sea itself, the shore fascinates us who return
to it, the place of our dim ancestral beginnings. In the
recurrent rhythms of tides and surf and in the varied
life of the tide lines there is the obvious attraction
of movement and chance and beauty. There is also,
I am convinced, a deeper fascination born of inner
meaning and significance.

    When we go down to the low-tide line, we enter
a world that is as old as the earth itself—the primeval
meeting place of the elements of earth and water, a
place of compromise and conflict and eternal change.
For us as living creatures it has a special meaning as
an area in or near which some entity that could be
distinguished as Life first drifted in shallow waters—
reproducing, evolving, yielding that endlessly varied

stream of living things that has surged through time
and space to occupy the earth.

—Rachel Carson

The ocean is one of the delights for the human eye.
The seashore is a theater of fluency. When the mind
is entangled it is soothing to walk by the seashore,
to let the rhythm of the ocean inside you. The ocean
disentangles the netted mind. Everything loosens and
comes back to itself. The false divisions are relieved,
released, and healed.

—John O'Donohue

John O'Donohue writes in one of his poems about his desire to
live like a river, "carried by the surprise / of its own unfolding." In
this way, the element of water is similar to the energy of wind or air
that blows freely where it will. Embracing the gifts of wind and water invites us into a way of being that asks us to hold less tightly to
our carefully constructed plans. It offers us a path of listening and
responding to the movement in a given moment, of living our way
into the unknown. The poet Rilke invites us into the flow of water as
well, encouraging us to give freely from who we are. Water beckons
us into the sacred flow of life. We are asked to pour ourselves out,
trusting that in this act we will be refilled.

There is something about the sea that draws me to it. When I
am able to spend several days by the water, something always shifts
in me. I am able to hear the Holy One more clearly through the
rhythms of waves and tides and the vast mystery of the ocean. A couple of years ago I rented a tiny cottage over the winter season along
the Hood Canal, which is a channel of water that runs between the
Kitsap and Olympic peninsulas in the state of Washington. I would
spend part of my week at the hermitage, as I called it, and part back
home in Seattle. There were many gifts to that time: the space to listen, the beauty of the beach, time to simply be. Perhaps the greatest

gift of all was becoming aware of the rise and fall of the tides each day. The cottage was on a beach that was accessible only at low tide. So the tide table became my constant companion. I would have to plan my walk each day by its schedule, making sure to leave enough hours to amble along the shores and return before the water rose and covered the sand once more.

One of the things I discovered there was the importance of following my own rhythms. Listening to my internal rising and falling was sheer gift—I ate when I was hungry, slept when I was tired, and wrote when I was moved to work. I entered into the sacred flow of my soul's longing and in the process connected to the sacred flow that runs through the heart of everything. So often we try to force ourselves into schedules that don't fit us, that leave us exhausted. Certainly we need to work and earn money for food and shelter, but what might happen if one day each week you released the hold a schedule has on your life? What if you had a Sabbath whose main purpose was to free you from the external demands of time and allowed you to see the rhythms of time as gift and invitation to a more intentional and less controlled way of being?

I know I can get so caught up in planning, in trying to have some measure of control in my life, that I can forget about the process itself. Spirituality is primarily about process, about the journey itself rather than the end goal. We are invited to tend to and celebrate the process of our becoming. The tides teach us to witness our own rising and falling, just like the sun's rising and setting does, and to make space for the movement of both in our lives. As I discover while watching the tides, both are necessary. Our culture tells us to rise and rise and rise until we collapse in exhaustion. The ocean tells me otherwise and offers me wisdom for a way to live that is renewing and organic.

Being organic means allowing your own process to unfold. It means allowing the rise and fall of your own energy and desires. It means to hold plans and expectations lightly and notice where your energy and prayer are taking you. It means being open to the subtle ways that God shapes and transforms us moment by moment, listening deeply for the call of the Spirit leading us forward into our lives. This kind of awareness of what simply *is* in a given moment is a means of discovery. In listening, we discover new things about ourselves and about who God is for us. We encounter our stumbling blocks and resistances, our joys and hopes, our fears, what makes us feel passionate, vital, and alive. Welcome them all in as wise guides.

In our prayer, being organic means trusting in what is emerging. Trusting that what comes next will be revealed in its own time, in God's time, which is always much slower than our own hopes. It means waiting for the tide to pull back and discover what treasures lay hidden in the sand: oyster, clam, crab, seaweed, stone, driftwood, tumbled glass. The work of the universe unfolds gently, never rushed. A baby takes nine months to form in the womb; imagine what kind of work and time the sacred art of living requires.

In *Anam Cara*, John O'Donohue writes about honoring the voice and rhythms of the deep self, that place where the mystics tell us God dwells.

> Spirituality is the art of transfiguration. We should not force ourselves to change by hammering our lives into any pre-determined shape. We do not need to operate according to the idea of a predetermined program or plan for our lives. Rather, we need to practice a new art of attention to the inner rhythm of our days and lives. . . . If you work with a different rhythm, you will come easily and naturally home to yourself. Your soul knows the geography of your own destiny. Your soul alone has the map of your future, therefore you can trust this indirect, oblique side of yourself. . . . If you attend to yourself and seek to come into your presence, you will find exactly the right rhythm for your life. (57–58)

Allow the rhythms of the sea to shape your prayers.

FOR REFLECTION

- What are the natural rhythms of your life?
- How does your current schedule force you to work in opposition to how your body wants to move and be?

- Where in your life do you feel the invitation to embrace the sacred flow of things?

- Where are you invited to surrender to the flow of the river in your life?

- What are the places in your life of ebbing and rising?

PRAYING WITH FLOWING WATER

- Keep a bowl of water or a shell on your altar to remember the element of water in your prayer. Anne Morrow Lindbergh in her book *Gift from the Sea* contemplates a shell and asks, "What is the shape of my life?" Take a walk along the beach and look for a shell that captures your attention; ask what its shape might be telling you about your life.

- Spend some time by the sea, paying attention to the rise and fall of the tides. Honor what is rising and falling within you. Listen to what the sound of the waves evokes within you. Take time to free-write in a journal in response.

- Take a retreat for at least a couple of days where your only task is to listen to the rhythms of your own body. Notice when you are hungry, when you want to sleep, when you want to go for a walk, when you long for sitting in stillness. See if you can follow your instinct and intuition, and notice what you discover about yourself and your own rising and falling.

- At dusk offer a prayer for the time of transition from day to night, from light to dark. Stand facing the west in honor of the setting sun, and embrace the awareness that you have your own limits, that each day of life reflects the rising and falling of the tides and of your own breath, and that one day there will be that last fall into death.

- Spend time at the rich shoreline where water and earth meet, exploring tidal pools, and reflecting on the in-between spaces of your own life.

Living Water

Sweet eternal will of God, you've taught us how to
find you. If we asked our kind, loving Savior and most
merciful Father, "How can we find you?" God would
tell us: "If you want to find and experience the fruit
of My will, always live in the cell of your soul." Now
the cell is a well of both earth and water. We can
understand the earth to be our own poverty when we
recognize that of ourselves we're nothing. That's why
we must admit our being comes to us from God. He
is living water. Let us plunge into this well!

—Catherine of Siena

Everyone who thirsts, come to the waters.

—Isaiah 55:1a

Let everyone who is thirsty come.
Let anyone who wishes take the water of life as gift.

—Revelation 22:17

Let anyone who is thirsty come to me and let the one
  who believes in me drink.
As the scripture has said: "Out of the believer's heart
  shall flow rivers of living water."

—John 7:38

My soul thirsts for you.

—Psalm 63:1

> There is in all things an inexhaustible sweetness and
> purity, a silence that is a fount of action and joy. It
> rises up in wordless gentleness and flows out to me
> from the unseen roots of all created being, welcoming
> me tenderly, saluting me with indescribable humility.
> This is at once my own being, my own nature, and
> the Gift of my Creator's Thought and Art within
> me, speaking as Hagia Sophia, speaking as my sister,
> Wisdom.
>
> —Thomas Merton

The metaphor of thirst is repeated several times throughout scripture. We have all had times when our hearts have felt dry and arid, when our prayer felt distant and disconnected from our Source. We have all been thirsty on a physical level, and we know how incredible that first drink of water tastes as it passes our lips. This is just like our spiritual lives, say the sacred texts. In the midst of our own desert experiences, when the dryness abates and God rushes back into our lives, it is as the living water that satisfies us as nothing else can. This living water revitalizes us, energizes us, quenches our deep thirst in a lasting way.

In the gospel story of the Samaritan woman at the well, Jesus encounters a woman at the height of the day's heat. She is thirsting desperately for God. When I lived in Sacramento for a few years, at our parish was a woman who would tell that story from the perspective of the Samaritan woman herself. She would carry us through the journey of her own desolation and dryness, she would invite us into the desert of the experience of her profound longing. The moment when Jesus offers her living water, she savored that experience with us and invited us to enter into it with her, imagining what it would be like to be offered that gift.

Another kind of living water is the tears that flow from our eyes. In the Christian tradition, tears have often been looked upon as a gift. John Cassian and St. John Climacus, saints of the Christian East, considered tears to be of great importance, especially tears of compunction. These are the tears of sorrow we shed over having gone far away from God. St. Ignatius of Loyola mentions his own tears again and again in his diary. Most of his tears, however, were tears of joy, in response to the tremendous grace of God he experienced in his life and which he described as "affectionate awe." He cried so much he feared he might go blind.

Scientists categorize the kinds of tears we cry both according to their purpose and to their chemical makeup. Basal tears are the tears that flow continuously to keep our eyes moist. Reflex tears are those that occur when something gets into our eyes and needs to be flushed out. Psychic tears, those that arise from an emotional response, have an entirely different chemical composition. They contain significantly more proteins, potassium, manganese, as well as hormones connected to our emotional state. There are some scientists who hypothesize that through the act of crying we are eliminating hormones and proteins that generate the feelings that created the sadness in the first place. There is a cleansing and renewing power to crying. Tears of compunction are those moments we cry with sorrow over our own woundedness and move us closer to the God who is the great Healer of all. Beauty and moments of grace also can move us to tears. The saints describe all of these as the grace of tears, a kind of living water that streams from our eyes in response to the most powerful moments of our lives.

FOR REFLECTION

- Where in your life are you longing for renewal of living water?

- Can you allow your holy tears of sorrow and joy to flow?

PRAYING WITH LIVING WATER

- Take some time to reflect in your journal about times when your soul felt parched and thirsty. See if you can re-enter that experience in your imagination. Remember and savor the movement from dry and desolate to quenched and full of living water.

- Use the method of Ignatian Contemplation with the story of the woman at the well. Open to John's gospel (4:1–42) and read the passage through slowly. Then set it aside and, closing your eyes, allow yourself to move into your imagination and step into the scene. Engage all of your senses to become aware of what is happening around you. Notice the sights, sounds, smells, tastes, and feelings. Watch as Jesus interacts with the Samaritan woman. See the expressions on both of their faces as they move through their conversation. Take in that moment when Jesus offers her living water and she accepts and is able to receive this gift into her life. End with a colloquy with Jesus about where you would like to have living water poured into your own life.

- Pray to receive the gift of tears. Take some time to get in touch with a loss you have experienced that has gone ungrieved. Allow yourself an hour or so to connect with the feelings this loss evokes in you. Give yourself permission to cry if tears rise up, and honor these tears as expressions of the Spirit moving through you. The next time you feel moved to tears, whether for joy or sadness, see if you can allow yourself the freedom to enter into this spontaneous gift and offer your tears to God, remembering the psalmist's words that God "gathers our tears into a vial" (56:9).

Holy Wells, Desert Springs, and Fountains

They feast on the abundance of your house;
and you give them to drink from your river of
delights.
For with you is the fountain of life, and in your light
we see light.

—Psalm 36:8–9

He turns a desert into pools of water, a parched land
  into springs of water.

—Psalm 107:35

I will open rivers on the bare heights,
and fountains in the midst of the valleys;
I will make the wilderness a pool of water,
and the dry land springs of water.

—Isaiah 41:18

This happened on that most sacred night in which
the sweet dew of divine grace gently showered the
world. It was the night when the heavens had already
dropped celestial rain as I meditated in the court of
the monastery.

—St. Gertrude the Great

God will guide you continually,
and satisfy your needs in parched places,
and make your bones strong;
and you shall be like a watered garden,
like a spring of water,
whose waters never fail.

—Isaiah 58:11

Don't say, don't say there is no water
to solace the dryness at our hearts.
I have seen

the fountain springing out of the rock wall
and you drinking there. And I too
before your eyes

found footholds and climbed
to drink the cool water.

The woman of that place, shading her eyes,
frowned as she watched—but not because
she grudged the water,

only because she was waiting
to see we drank our fill and were
refreshed.

Don't say, don't say there is no water.
That fountain is there among its scalloped
green and gray stones,

it is still there and always there
with its quiet song and strange power
to spring in us,

up and out through the rock.

—Denise Levertov

Have you been to one of those places by the seashore where
there is an opening under the rocks and, as a wave comes in, water spouts upward all of a sudden? Our creative energy is often like
that, like an unexpected spring or fountain within the heart. Often
it comes like the surprising gift of water in the desert or out through
the hard, stony edges of the heart. These waves of creative energy can cause us some hesitancy, some worry that it might be over
too soon, or some uncertainty about when it might return. This response comes from a place of scarcity, a sense that there might not
be enough. I have long wrestled with what is enough for me. Yet
somehow, because I have discovered this spring bursting forth again
and again, I no longer live in fear of when this time of abundance
will wane. Perhaps it comes from having lived through enough ebbing and flowing to know that when the creative energy dissipates,

it means I am being called back inward to rest and renew. I need to go drink my fill again or rest into the healing waters. And when the surge is rising, I dance in its splendor and joy.

There are places where mineral hot springs bubble beneath the earth's surface and are considered to be sites of healing. One such place out in the desert of New Mexico is called Ojo Caliente. *Ojo* means "oasis in the desert," and *caliente* means "hot." It is a place that has been considered sacred for hundreds of years, perhaps even longer. There in a dry and parched landscape emerge healing waters, and people travel long distances to gather there. There are multiple pools, each with a different mineral content and temperature, recommended to treat various health issues. Those who soak in these waters often find the experience akin to being held in a warm and loving embrace, coaxing one out of one's places of tension and distress.

Across the landscape of Ireland are nearly three thousand holy wells venerated in Celtic tradition as sacred places where water surges forth. When I traveled to Ireland, I visited the site of St. Brigid's well, in county Clare, a popular place of pilgrimage. In order to see it, the visitor must enter a stone well-house. The air is damp inside, saturated by the water that flows down one wall. Alongside the other walls, many pilgrims have left offerings, votives, and rosaries in this sacred place.

FOR REFLECTION

- What practices help you to experience the fountain flowing within you?

- What are the ways in which you experience the rise and fall of your creative energies?

- Do you live in fear that there will not be more inspiration?

- In this season are you being called to renew yourself or extend your gifts into this world?

PRAYING WITH HEALING WATER

- Begin your time of prayer by finding your pulse and reflecting on the life-giving blood and water being pumped through your system. You might try practicing centering prayer by using this image of water surging through your body like a fountain as the anchor that keeps your attention on God.

- Spend some time by a fountain, listening to the flow of the water and contemplating its invitation for your own life. Pay attention to those places where water wants to surge up and offer its refreshment. Make note of the streams, rivers, and other water sources near you as places for prayer.

- Reflect on the holy wells and oases in your life. What are those experiences and people who bring you a sense of renewal? How might you express thanks for these and cultivate their presence in your daily life?

Viriditas

> Opus Verbi viriditas. [The work of the Word is greenness.]
>
> —Hildegard of Bingen

> Fire of the Holy Spirit,
> life of the life of every creature,
> holy are you in giving life to forms . . .
> Rivers spring forth from the waters
> earth wears her green vigor.
>
> —Hildegard of Bingen

The rain I am in is not like the rain of the cities.
It fills the woods with an immense and confused
sound. It covers the flat roof of the cabin and porch
with insistent and controlled rhythms. And I listen,
because it reminds me again and again that the
whole world runs by rhythms I have not yet learned
to recognize, rhythms that are not those of the
engineer.

   I came up here from the monastery last night,
sloshing through the cornfield, said Vespers, and
put some oatmeal on the Coleman stove for supper.
It boiled over while I was listening to the rain and
toasting a piece of bread at the log fire. The night
became very dark. The rain surrounded the whole
cabin with its enormous virginal myth, a whole world
of meaning, of secrecy, of silence, of rumor. Think
of it: all that speech pouring down, selling nothing,
judging nobody, drenching the thick mulch of
dead leaves, soaking the trees, filling the gullies and
crannies of the wood with water, washing out the
places where men have stripped the hillside! What
a thing it is to sit absolutely alone, in the forest, at
night, cherished by this wonderful, unintelligible,
perfectly innocent speech, the most comforting
speech in the world, the talk that rain makes by itself
all over the ridges, and the talk of the watercourses
everywhere in the hollows!

—Thomas Merton

   The twelfth-century mystic and Benedictine abbess Hildegard
of Bingen coined the term *viriditas* (literally *greenness*), by which she
meant the greening power of God. Hildegard used the term to refer
to the literal reality of the earth's greening and fecundity, but also
to the soul's greening. The moister and greener a soul is, the more

93

deeply it is connected to its sacred source. In winter, the earth is drenched with rain and greenness, inviting us to consider the dry places of our own souls, needing the gift of vigor and life.

The natural world is not inert, but rather is filled with life and power. Hildegard writes of the "green finger of God." This greening vitality is a manifestation of God's activity in the world. Hildegard's emphasis on greenness symbolizes the inner dynamism of life in all its burgeoning growth, vibrancy, freshness, and fecundity as emanating from the life-creating power of God. It expresses her vision of God as the source, sustainer, and energizer of all life—cosmic, human, angelic, and celestial.

We might say that viriditas is God's love, energizing the world, making it living and fruitful. Nothing exists without viriditas because nothing exists without God loving it and wanting it to exist. For Hildegard, the universality of greenness shows us the universality of God's love. God is known through the viriditas of God's creatures. Earth's burgeoning life depends on not only rainfall but ultimately the living energy of God. The soul knows its health by its own degree of moistness and how it receives this sacred, nourishing water from God.

I first encountered Hildegard's writings while in graduate school, and I thought I understood this greenness of which she wrote. Then I moved to Seattle and discovered depths of viriditas previously unrevealed to me. In the Northwest winters, I witness the subtle, slow waves of velvety moss that spread up tree trunks and across sidewalks. I once heard a saying on the radio that in the Northwest if moss isn't growing on your north side, you are moving too fast. I shared this with the driver of an airport shuttle once as we made our way through blankets of thick rain. "You can tell an outsider made that up," he responded, "because around here moss grows on all sides." And this is indeed true, much to the chagrin of homeowners who discover moss everywhere. I, however, fell in love with this sign of green, persistent hope.

FOR REFLECTION

- How are you being invited to reinvigorate yourself?
- How might you give yourself the gift of greenness?

- What practices help to cultivate your vibrancy and verdancy?

PRAYING WITH WATER AS A SOURCE OF GREENNESS

- Take a contemplative walk through a forest or nearby park, and pay attention to the appearance of the color green in all of its manifestations. How many shades of green can you identify? Appreciate the work of God through the power of greening. What do the myriad ways the world is made green reflect about your own spirit? Reflect on the places you want to invite God's greening power to touch you more deeply, and then pray for this gift.

- Take time each day to do another modified version of the Ignatian prayer of Examen. In the evening, reflect back on your experiences of the previous day and ask: Where today did I experience God's greening, enlivening energy? What is the felt experience in my body? Take some time to offer gratitude for this experience. Then ask: Where today did my life feel dry, lifeless, or arid? What is the felt experience of this in my body? Take some time to offer forgiveness to anyone who might have contributed to this experience. Then invite God's living water into those places.

Baptism and Blessing

I do not want you to be unaware, brothers, that our ancestors were all under the cloud and all passed through the sea, and all of them were baptized into Moses in the cloud and in the sea. All ate the same spiritual food, and all drank the same spiritual drink, for they drank from a spiritual rock that followed them, and the rock was the Christ.

—1 Corinthians 10:1–4

Amen, amen, I say to you, no one can enter the
kingdom of God without being born of water and
Spirit.

—John 3:5

The people quarreled with Moses, and said, "Give us
water to drink." Moses said to them, "Why do you
quarrel with me? Why do you test the Lord?" But
the people thirsted there for water; and the people
complained against Moses and said, "Why did you
bring us out of Egypt, to kill us and our children and
livestock with thirst?" So Moses cried out to the Lord,
"What shall I do with this people? They are almost
ready to stone me." The Lord said to Moses, "Go
on ahead of the people, and take some of the elders
of Israel with you; take in your hand the staff with
which you struck the Nile, and go. I will be standing
there in front of you on the rock at Horeb. Strike the
rock, and water will come out of it, so that the people
may drink." Moses did so, in the sight of the elders
of Israel. He called the place Massah and Meribah,
because the Israelites quarreled and tested the Lord,
saying, "Is the Lord among us or not?"

—Exodus 17:1–7

In those days Jesus came from Nazareth of Galilee
and was baptized by John in the Jordan. And just
as he was coming up out of the water, he saw the
heavens torn apart and the Spirit descending like a

dove on him. And a voice came from heaven, "You
are my Son, the Beloved; with you I am well pleased."

—Mark 1:9–11

The voice of the Lord cries over the waters, saying:
Come all you, receive the Spirit of wisdom, the Spirit
of understanding, the Spirit of the fear of God, even
Christ who is made manifest.

Today the nature of water is sanctified. Jordan is
divided in two, and turns back the stream of its
waters, beholding the Master being baptized. As a
man Thou didst come to that river, O Christ our
King, and dost hasten O Good One, to receive the
baptism of a servant at the hands of the Forerunner
(John), because of our sins, O Lover of Man.

—Hymn of the Great Blessing of Waters

At the feast of the Epiphany, the Eastern Orthodox church holds
the Great Blessing of Water. As the hymn of the feast is sung, the
celebrant immerses the cross in the water three times and then pro-
ceeds to sprinkle the water in the four directions of the world.

At the entrance of churches we find fonts of holy water to bless
ourselves. There we also find baptismal fonts flowing with holy water to initiate members into the Christian community and to invite
them, and ourselves, into a spiritual rebirth. Jesus was baptized to
initiate his own mission. He ended his earthly mission by washing
the feet of his disciples the night before he was crucified.

When I reach the end of one of those very long days and my
body is tired and my spirit is weary, I take a bath to allow myself to
be blessed by healing water. I walk into the kitchen to fill up two
large pots with water and put them on the stove to heat. Then I head
into the bathroom and begin to fill the tub. We live in a condo with
space only for a small water heater, not quite enough to fill the tub,

so this routine has become part of my nightly ritual. "I can't believe you live in the heart of Seattle and you have to heat water on the stove for your bath," my aunt teases when she calls to check in with me from her house in rural Maine with plenty of hot water. "What a pain that must be."

Truth be told, I don't mind at all. It's all a part of the process for me—these moments of preparation needed to enter this holy space of renewal each evening. Heating the water, running the faucet, pouring in some bath salts, telling my husband I'll be disappearing for an hour, turning off the phone ringer—all signal to me I am on the threshold of something sacred. This is one of my slowing-down spaces, of which we have too few in our busy lives. Here I can reflect on the cleansing power of water and, more deeply, on my baptismal vows that, in a sense, must be renewed daily.

FOR REFLECTION

- How might you bring the spirit of blessing into all that you do each day? What would it be like to quietly offer blessing over each act and person you encounter?

- Is there a place of sacred water near you that might be inviting you to spend some time?

- What does the sacrament of baptism mean for you?

- How are you being invited to become washed clean?

PRAYING WITH CLEANSING WATER

- Find a small bowl made of glass or ceramic, one that in color or design evokes the qualities of water for you. Begin your time of prayer by dipping your fingers into the water and blessing yourself. Call to mind the water that supports your body and covers the earth. Acknowledge this great gift. Offer prayers for cleansing and renewal and to surrender to the flow of the Spirit in the day ahead.

- End your day by taking a bath and make it a sacred act of renewal. Pray for those who do not have access to fresh water, and remember your connection to people across the world who consider water to be a sacred element. Allow this act to be a renewal of your own baptismal vows.

- Turn the mundane into something holy. Each time you wash the dishes, your car, or the floor, allow yourself to be completely mindful of the moment. Give thanks for this opportunity to be washed clean.

Lectio Divina with Water

Preparation

Find a place where you can contemplate the element of water, perhaps sitting by a lake or river or on the beach by the ocean. You can also engage in this practice with a bowl of water in front of you or while taking a bath. Find a comfortable position, shifting your body so you feel relaxed and open. Take as much time as you need to turn inward and settle into stillness. With the in-breath, breathe in an awareness of the fluid and flowing qualities of the Spirit; with the out-breath, breathe out all that distracts you from this time of prayer. Allow your breath to gather your awareness and move you more deeply inward to a place of stillness.

Reading God's Word

Become aware of the water before you. Notice the aspect of water that invites you or stirs you, whether the color or motion or some quality that captures your gaze. Listen for the way God might be calling you to deeper attention to water this day. Keep listening until you have a sense of which manifestation of water is inviting you, and then spend some time in appreciation of it.

Reflecting on God's Word

Allow the quality of water that has captured your attention to unfold in your memory and imagination. Notice what feelings, memories, or images arise for you. Allow the Spirit to expand your capacity for listening and to open you to a fuller experience of this element at work in the world. Begin to notice where its qualities touch your life. What do you see, hear, touch, or remember? What is evoked in you? Allow it to interact with your thoughts, your hopes, your memories, your desires. Spend some time tending these movements within you.

Responding to God's Word

After a time of resting in what the element of water evokes in you, you will be moved to deeper insight and a desire to respond and say yes to God. When this time comes, attend to the way the unfolding of your memories, images, and feelings connects with the context and situation of your life right now. How does it relate to what you have heard and seen this day? How does it connect with what is happening at home, at work, in your leisure time? Take an extended time of exploring this connection. How is God present to you there? Is God calling you to anything in your present circumstances? Is there a challenge presented here? Address your response to God in whatever way seems appropriate.

Resting with God's Word

Finally, simply rest in the presence of the One who has spoken to you intimately and personally through the gift of water. Rest in the silence of God's loving embrace and allow your heart to be moved to gratitude for this time of prayer.

More Water Quotations for Prayer

I live by a creek, Tinker Creek, in a valley in Virginia's Blue Ridge. . . . The creeks—Tinker and Carvin's— are an active mystery, fresh every minute. Theirs is the mystery of the continuous creation and all that providence implies: the uncertainty of vision, the

horror of the fixed, the dissolution of the present,
the intricacy of beauty, the pressure of fecundity,
the elusiveness of the free, and the flawed nature of
perfection.

—Annie Dillard

Consider also the grand spectacle of the sea, robing
herself in different colors, like garments: sometimes
green, and that in so many different shades;
sometimes purple; sometimes blue.

—St. Augustine of Hippo

And how would God be known as the Eternal One if
brilliance did not emerge from God? For there is not
creature without some kind of radiance—whether it
be greenness, seeds, buds, or another kind of beauty.

—Hildegard of Bingen

Blessing of Water

Spirit of Living Water,
You hold all of creation in your womb
And spring us forward onto the earth at birth.

Spirit of the Tides,
Remind me of the rise and fall of your rhythms
So that I may discover them deep within my own being.

Spirit of Greenness,
Bring moistness and vigor to my life
So that I might savor the experience of your energy
Moving through me out into the world.

Blessings of water be upon me.
May I be carried by the flow of the great river of life.
May I discover a hidden spring within, gushing forth,
May I be carried to the shores of the sacred and renewed.

chapter four

Sister Earth

All praise be Yours, my God, through Sister Earth, our mother,
Who feeds us in her sovereignty and produces
Various fruits and colored flowers and herbs.

—St. Francis of Assisi

Deep peace of the quiet earth to you, who,
herself unmoving, harbors the movements
and facilitates the life of the ten thousand creatures,
while resting contented, stable, tranquil.
Deep peace of the quiet earth to you!

—Celtic Prayer

Earth and Creation

God said,
"Come no closer!
Remove the sandals from your feet,
for the place on which you are standing
is holy ground."

—Exodus 3:5

This earth we are riding keeps trying to tell us
something with its continuous scripture of leaves.

—William Stafford

O Earth! O Earth! When will we hear you sing,
Arising from our grassy hills?
And say: "The dark is gone, and Day
Laughs like a bridegroom in His tent, the lovely sun!
His tent the sun!
His tent the smiling sky!"
How long we wait, with minds as dim as ponds,
While stars swim slowly homeward in the waters of
    our west?
O Earth! When will we hear you sing?

—Thomas Merton

Pray the prayer of action, which is the fragrant
flowering of the soul.

—Catherine of Siena

Glory be to God for dappled things—
For skies of couple-colour as a brinded cow;
For rose-moles all in stipple upon trout that swim;
Fresh-firecoal chestnut-falls; finches' wings;
Landscape plotted and pieced—fold, fallow, and
    plough;
And all trades, their gear and tackle and trim.

All things counter, original, spare, strange;
Whatever is fickle, freckled (who knows how?)
With swift, slow; sweet, sour; adazzle, dim; He
    fathers forth whose beauty is past change:
Praise him.

           —Gerard Manley Hopkins

Love all God's creation, the whole and every grain of
sand in it. Love every leaf, every ray of God's light.
Love the animals, love the plants, love everything.
If you love everything, you will perceive the divine
mystery in things. When you are left alone, pray.
Love to throw yourself on the earth and kiss it. Kiss
the earth and love it with an unceasing, consuming
love.

           —Fyodor Dostoevsky

If we think of ourselves as coming out of the earth,
rather than having been thrown in here from
somewhere else, we see that we are the earth; we are
the consciousness of the earth. These are the eyes of
the earth. And this is the voice of the earth.

           —Joseph Campbell

In indigenous traditions, the element of earth is often associated with the direction of the north and the season of winter. The north is the place of the midnight moon, the time for sleep and renewal, for reflection and turning inward. Winter is a time of hibernation and conserving energy during the long cold months and dark days. Earth comes in many different forms—soil, rock, clay, sand, dust, mud, mineral, stone. Earth stands for what is material and solid in our being. It is the element our bodies are made of, breathed into, lit on fire, with blood and water flowing through our veins. It becomes the container for the other elements. Earth as an element symbolizes the necessities and commitments of our lives. It represents our limitations as well as our possibilities. The word *humility* comes from the root *humus*, which means *earth*. Humility means knowing both our limits and our gifts intimately. It means being in touch with our own earthiness. When we are deeply rooted, our branches can reach far and wide.

When Jesus walked the earth, he used metaphors of soil and harvest to deliver his message, especially in his parables. Those listening to him would have been intimately connected to the earth, dependent on her fruitfulness. He used images of soil and seed, of sheep, of field and treasure, of pearl and trees, often to describe the kingdom of heaven. Jesus is telling us that this kingdom is not some far off, unreachable place, but here to be discovered in the midst of everyday life.

We live in a time when we are largely disconnected from the gifts of the earth's cycles, rhythms, and seasons, which have so much wisdom to offer us about the nature of change. The forms of earth have much to teach us about our own internal landscapes:

> Each of the great forms that Earth takes—mountains and hills and plains and valleys and meadows and steppes and swamps and marshes and deserts and forests and jungles and savannas and beaches and islands—each of these geographies we transmute to geobiographies of our own personal journey across time and circumstance. We too rise up, we ascend, we fall, only to rise and fall over and over, until we are leveled and become one again with the single mantle that is the resting ground and birthing ground of it all. The meanings we ascribe to the trajectory

of our lives are the same ones we observe in the fate of the Earth. The finite summit of the mountain's peak, the river's final arrival to the sea, the clearing in the depths of the woods, serve as exemplars and as metaphors for the often steep and uncertain and perilous journey that is our life. (Peter London, *Drawing Closer to Nature*, 202)

I love that word London evokes—"geobiographies." It speaks to me of honoring the profound role of place in our internal landscapes and spiritual journeys. What are the places and contours of your landscape that have shaped your own life and practice?

As I wrote this chapter, while reflecting on earth, I held a stone in my hand and then placed it next to my keyboard to help connect me to the groundedness of earth. I pray that I might be rooted deeply in fertile soil and the words I write bear fruit.

In this chapter you are invited to explore the impact of earth on your own prayer and spiritual life: through the tree of life, holy mountains, gardens, limitations, feasting and communion, and earth's creatures.

Getting in Touch with the Earth

- Find a topographical map of your area to learn the geography of where you live and the places of elevation.

- Walk barefoot through the grass or go hiking in the woods.

- Visit your local farmers' market.

- Give thanks for nourishment, and consider giving to a hunger relief organization such as Bread for the World (www.bread.org).

Tree of Life

Picture in your mind a tree whose roots are watered by an ever-flowing fountain that becomes a great and living river to water the garden of the entire church.

From the trunk of this tree, imagine that there are growing twelve branches that are adorned with leaves, flowers and fruit. Imagine that these leaves are a most effective medicine to prevent and cure every kind of sickness. Let the flowers be beautiful with the radiance of every color and perfumed with the sweetness of every fragrance. Imagine that there are twelve fruits, offered to God's servants to be tasted so that when they eat it, they may always be satisfied, yet never weary of the taste.

—St. Bonaventure

I am like a green olive tree in the house of God.

—Psalm 52:8

Out of the ground the LORD God made various trees grow that were delightful to look at and good for food, with the tree of life in the middle of the garden and the tree of the knowledge of good and bad.

—Genesis 2:9

I am the Vine and you are the branches.

—John 15:5

After I'd received the body of Christ, I saw that my soul was like a tree fastening its roots in the wound at the right side of Jesus. Then in some new and wonderful way I felt a marvelous sap—the goodness of the humanity and divinity of Jesus Christ— transfusing itself through this wound, as through a root, penetrating into all my branches and fruit and

leaves. Surging through my soul, then, the goodness
of Christ's whole life shone more brightly, like gold
shining through crystal.

—St. Gertrude the Great

How surely gravity's law,
strong as an ocean current,
takes hold of even the strongest thing
and pulls it toward the heart of the world.

Each thing—
each stone, blossom, child—
is held in place.
Only we, in our arrogance,
push out beyond what we belong to
for some empty freedom.

If we surrendered
to earth's intelligence
we could rise up rooted, like trees.

Instead we entangle ourselves
in knots of our own making
and struggle, lonely and confused.

So, like children, we begin again
to learn from the things,
because they are in God's heart;
they have never left him.

This is what the things can teach us:
to fall,
patiently to trust our heaviness.
Even a bird has to do that
before he can fly.

—Rainer Maria Rilke

The tree of life is a dominant motif in various religious traditions and mythologies, as well as a mystical concept that points to the interconnectedness of all creation. It appears in the second creation story of Genesis, in the garden of Eden, and is a significant symbol for both Jewish and Christian traditions.

I love the image of the scripture of leaves that Stafford offers—what if we were to consider the changing trees as a sacred text where the Holy One is revealed to us in new ways each season? What if we followed the invitation of each season—spring's emerging, summer's fullness, autumn's release, and winter's rest? Morning walks are a part of my daily spiritual practice. I walk to be present to the natural world while living in the heart of a city. I am fortunate there are parks nearby with beautiful, elegant, and noble trees with which I go to spend time. In the book *The Secret Life of Trees*, Colin Tudge writes:

> Perhaps this is why we feel so drawn to trees. Groves of redwoods and beeches are often compared to the naves of great cathedrals: the silence; the green, filtered, numinous light. A single banyan, each with its multitude of trunks, is like a temple or mosque—a living colonnade. But the metaphor should be the other way around. The cathedrals and mosques emulate the trees. The trees are innately holy.

In Northern California, Muir Woods is an old-growth coastal redwood forest. It has a section called "Cathedral Grove" where the average age of the trees is 500 to 800 years, and the oldest is more than 1,200 years old and 258 feet tall. Standing in this place, I experienced a sense of awe that I have felt in great cathedrals and other sacred spaces. Such experiences can remind us of Jesus' parable of the sower and of the seed that fell on good soil, "growing up and increasing" (Mk 4:8).

FOR REFLECTION

- Where do you experience yourself rooted in the Earth?

- Where do you need more of a sense of grounding?

- How might you honor the rhythms of the seasons more deeply?

PRAYING WITH THE GROUNDEDNESS OF EARTH

- Is there a particular tree that you love, maybe outside of your home or in a nearby park? If there isn't, go for a walk and see if you can discover one that might have something to teach you about the gifts of the earth. Observe it through the seasons with its changing leaves if it is deciduous or its constancy if it is evergreen.

- In the thirteenth century, St. Bonaventure, a Franciscan friar, wrote *The Tree of Life*, which is a prayerful meditation on the life of Christ. In it, Bonaventure invites his reader to imagine the tree as a metaphor for prayer. Take some time in prayer to read over his image (on pp. 107–108), and use it to enter into your imagination and visualize this lush tree, watered by the endless fountain and offering up every kind of beautiful flower and fruit with leaves that offer healing. Taste the fruit in your mind's eye, smell the fragrance, experience the healing offered.

- Wendell Berry, the great poet from Kentucky, suggests that the Bible is best read outdoors. Bring your Bible out to a beautiful spot under a tree and read the first creation story in Genesis slowly. Each time God says it is good, pause and breathe in that sense of the goodness of creation. Follow this reading with Psalm 104. Read it aloud as a response to the creation story and notice what stirs in you as you read the text in this outdoor setting.

Holy Mountain

Mountains and hills shall break out in song before you, and all the trees of the countryside shall clap their hands.

—Isaiah 55:12

The mountain opens its secrets only to those who
have the courage to challenge it. It demands sacrifice
and training. It requires you to leave the security
of the valleys but offers spectacular views from the
summit to those who have the courage to climb it.
Therefore it is a reality which strongly suggests the
journey of the spirit, called to lift itself up from the
earth to heaven, to meet God.

—Pope John Paul II

I came here to study hard things—rock mountain
and salt sea—and to temper my spirit on their edges.
"Teach me thy ways, O Lord" is, like all prayers,
a rash one, and one I cannot but recommend.
These mountains—Mount Baker and the Sisters
and Shuksan, the Canadian Coastal Range and the
Olympics on the peninsula—are surely the edge of
the known and comprehended world. . . . That they
bear their own unimaginable masses and weathers
aloft, holding them up in the sky for anyone to
see plain, makes them, as Chesterton said of the
Eucharist, only the more mysterious by their very
visibility and absence of secrecy.

—Annie Dillard

The pale flowers of the dogwood outside this
window are saints. The little yellow flowers that
nobody notices on the edge of that road are saints
looking up into the face of God. This leaf has it own
texture and its own pattern of veins and its own holy
shape, and the bass and trout hiding in the deep
pools of the river are canonized by their beauty and
their strength. The lakes hidden among the hills are

saints, and the sea too is a saint who praises God
without interruption in her majestic dance. The great,
gashed, half-naked mountain is another of God's
saints. There is no other like him. He is alone in his
own character; nothing else in the world ever did or
ever will imitate God in quite the same way. That is
his sanctity.

—Thomas Merton

O tall mountains
of confidence in God,
you never surrender when the Lord tests you!
Although you stand far away from me
as if in exile, all alone,
you remind me that
no armed power is strong enough to best you.
Your trust in God is wonderful!

—Hildegard of Bingen

One climbs a mountain drawn instinctively by the
magnetism of the highest point, as to a summit of
personal awareness, awareness of oneself as a point in
relation to as much of space as can be grasped within
maximal horizon. Thus a mountain top is one of the
most sensitive spots on earth.

—Tim Robinson

As a child, my family would go to the Tyrolean mountains in my
father's native Austria. I remember with such fondness the preparation of gear, putting on the proper socks and boots, packing a ruck-
sack with lunch and drink, and carrying my hiking stick. At each
summit we reached, I would attach a new medallion to my stick. I

loved the collection that spanned it and indicated those places to which I had taken the difficult journey. I continue to enjoy such journeys today. I can remember so clearly that crisp day while I was on retreat at the Columbia River Gorge, which marks the border between Oregon and Washington States. Mount Hood appeared brilliant against the pale blue sky, where the day before it had been shrouded in mist. I was filled with awe and felt connected to the wonder this sight must have inspired in native peoples walking this land long ago, and why this mountain would have been considered sacred. Mountains have always been places of theophany—an encounter with holiness—such as Mount Sinai, where Moses received God's laws and saw God's face; or Mount Tabor, where Jesus became transfigured before his disciples. The Northwest is dotted with these reminders of the majestic nature of the divine. Mount Rainier and Mount Baker hover above the Northwest landscape and evoke a sense of awe on those days when they are not hidden by our typically grey skies. The days on which they are revealed are treasured among those who pay attention.

In scripture, mountains and hills are referred to more often than any other geographical feature. Noah's ark came to rest on a mountain; God tested Abraham on a mountain; Jesus goes to the Mount of Olives to pray. Mountains stretch our imaginations upward in celebration of a transcendent God who creates with such glory and majesty.

In the fifth century, St. Patrick went up the sacred mountain, now called Croagh Patrick, and fasted at the summit for forty days. It is now known as Ireland's pilgrimage mountain because more than one million people each year come to climb it and connect with the longing for God that carried St. Patrick to its summit. This mountain had already been sacred to ancient Celtic people, who celebrated the harvest festival at this site.

The metaphor of ascent—climbing the holy mountain—is a dominant one in spiritual language. There is great challenge in rising higher and higher as the air for breath grows thinner and colder. Climbing mountains is a physical and spiritual goal. There is something about the image of ascension, reaching the highest peaks, and then taking in the perspective. We speak of "mountaintop experiences" as those that move us to awe and wonder, memorable moments where we transcended our narrow daily concerns.

FOR REFLECTION

- What is the closest holy mountain (or even hill) to where you live? What does it reveal to you about the nature of the sacred?

- What have been some of your own summit experiences?

- What are the gifts the Earth is waiting to offer you, when you pay attention?

- When was the last time you stood on the earth without your shoes and recognized it as holy ground?

PRAYING WITH EARTH TO LIFT OUR EYES UPWARD

- Earth is associated with the direction of the north and midnight. Try facing the north late at night, and explore what this direction might have to teach you about your own journey. The north is not simply a direction on the planet, but a direction in our own lives. Journey is a dominant metaphor, and an underlying assumption is that our journey takes us in a particular direction. What do you associate with the north? What qualities does the north evoke in you as you listen in the dark of night? What images come to mind?

- Begin your time of prayer by grounding your body and experiencing your rootedness in the earth. Notice the way the ground supports your entire body. Offer a prayer for the many gifts of nourishment the Earth provides. Take a moment to ask what you need to feel more grounded in your life, and honor the response that stirs within you. In *hatha* yoga there is a posture called mountain pose. In it you stand with your feet firmly planted on the ground, hip-width apart and your arms by your sides, feeling the strength of being in this place.

- Make a pilgrimage to a nearby holy mountain or other place of elevation. It may be just a few miles away or several hundred. Be intentional about the journey and pack your supplies well. As you climb, see if you can stay focused on each step rather than on the end goal. As you reach the top, take in the view. Appreciate the wide horizon before you.

- Collect stones out in nature—in the woods, at a river or beach—and place them on your altar. Take some time to hold each one and get in touch with its shape and texture. Stack them one on top of another to create a *cairn*, which is a Gaelic word for a human-made pile of stones serving as a landmark, often indicating the top of a mountain or a burial site. It indicates something sacred nearby.

Sacred Garden

Then the LORD God planted a garden in Eden, in the east, and he placed there the man whom he had formed.

—Genesis 2:8

You shall be like a watered garden.

—Isaiah 58:11

I have said on occasion that I think gardening is nearer to godliness than theology. . . . True gardeners are both iconographers and theologians insofar as these activities are the fruit of prayer "without ceasing." Likewise, true gardeners never cease to garden, not even in their sleep, because gardening is not just something they do. It is how they live.

—Vigen Guroian

He set before me the book of nature; I understood
how all the flowers he has created are beautiful, how
the splendor of the rose and the whiteness of the lily
do not take away the perfume of the little violet or the
delightful simplicity of the daisy. I understood that if
all flowers wanted to be roses, nature would lose her
springtime beauty, and the fields would no longer be
decked out with little wild flowers. And so it is in the
world of souls, Jesus' garden. . . . Perfection consists in
doing His will, in being what He wills us to be.

—St. Thérèse of Lisieux

You are an enclosed garden, my sister, my bride,
an enclosed garden, a fountain sealed.

You are a park that puts forth pomegranates,
with all choice fruits;

Nard and saffron, calamus and cinnamon,
with all kinds of incense;
Myrrh and aloes,
with all the finest spices.

You are a garden fountain, a well of water
flowing fresh from Lebanon.

Arise, north wind! Come, south wind!
blow upon my garden
that its perfumes may spread abroad.

Let my lover come to his garden
and eat its choice fruits.

—Song of Songs 4:12–16

A garden is a place where nature has been carefully cultivated by human hands—to varying degrees. Some gardens are meticulously kept, while others are left to grow more wildly like the ones in my old neighborhood in Berkeley. I would go on long morning walks and in the springtime it seemed as though every yard I passed had a wild gathering of flowers, some with tall sunflowers surrounded by patches of marigolds mixed with bluebells, others with a tumble of flowering vines weaving around rosebushes. Containers of fuchsia would hang off rails, looking slightly drunk from the sunshine. A gathering of bees and hummingbirds would flutter back and forth, drinking in the nectar offered.

Gardens can also be manicured and carefully planned, such as the ones spread across the city of Paris. Rows of flowers are planted neatly and spaced apart exactly. Bushes are trimmed into neat shapes, and even the fountains seem to flow in orderly fashion. There is comfort in the orderliness of such places, a soothing sense that wildness can be somehow contained within those planters.

A garden, then, is that earthy place in between the wild and the cultivated. Having always been a city dweller, I have not had the privilege of growing my own garden. But even the window boxes I have maintained have had their moments of wild surprise. There have been the nuts I discovered in the soil, buried by squirrels anticipating winter. The small green shoot taking root alongside the flowers I planted, sprouting out sideways.

Gardens are significant places in scripture. The second creation story of Genesis takes place in the idyllic garden of Eden, where out of the ground "the Lord made to grow every tree that is pleasant to the sight and good for food" (Gn 2:9). At the end of Jesus' life he goes to the garden of Gethsemane, at the foot of the Mount of Olives, among a grove of olive trees that still exists to this day. It is in this place where Jesus prays the whole night and is distressed so deeply that he sweats drops of blood. The garden was the site of one of his deepest prayers.

FOR REFLECTION

- What does your inner garden look like? Is it carefully ordered and cultivated or wild and unruly? What kinds of flowers grow there?

- What memories of gardens do you have? What role have they played in your life?

PRAYING WITH THE EARTH AS GARDEN

- Begin your own garden if you do not already have one. Even a small container with a plant will do if space does not allow something larger. Take time to dig your hands into the earth and feel the cool soil. Choose what you want to cultivate and grow with intention, and place the seeds gently below the surface. Watch each day with anticipation as the shoots begin to rise.

- Spend time in your garden or a public garden nearby as a place for prayer. Allow this to be the container for your deepest expressions of longing.

- Buy fresh flowers (or gather them from your garden), and place them in a vase indoors on your altar to remind you of the blossoming of the sacred in your life.

- Take a walk through your neighborhood as a journey of discovery. Watch for beautiful weeds, small hidden gardens, grass sprouting from concrete. Georgia O'Keeffe says that "seeing takes time." Take time to see what you might discover when you linger. Bring your camera with you to capture moments that you may not have noticed otherwise.

- Use the contemplative walk format below to guide your journey through nature as a sacred presence where God dwells.

CONTEMPLATIVE WALK

This is a slow, contemplative walk. Take your time and linger over each moment. There is no need to hurry. Allow the walk to take its own shape (you don't need to walk a long distance, perhaps only a few feet). Walk mindfully, keeping your awareness on your immediate surroundings or on your own breath as you walk. Walk slowly, heel to toe, enjoying each step as a gift.

Use this time to open to your experience of the moment. Walk without any particular goal in mind. Be receptive to each moment as it unfolds before you, holding it lightly in your awareness, bringing both intention and attention to this time.

- *Noticing:* Notice what is capturing your attention in the world around you. Notice your surroundings. As you walk, allow creation to speak to you. Notice what lies in the path before you. Notice what is inviting you to spend more time (what is drawing you), and accept the invitation. When your mind begins to wander, draw your awareness back to the present and what is happening now.

- *Wondering:* Focusing on the things you have noticed both in your body and in nature, you might want to begin to ask questions of it using the phrase beginning, "I wonder . . . ?" I wonder what it has to say to me? I wonder why this captures my attention? I wonder how this came into being? I wonder what this thing I have noticed has to do with my life? (You may wish to journal your responses or draw them.) Let the wondering draw you to a deeper sense of conversation with the holy presence.

- *Returning:* As you return, think about what has happened to you on this journey. What captured your attention? What are the questions and stirrings that linger with you?

Feasting and Communion

Taste and see that the Lord is good.

—Psalm 34:8

Jesus said to them, "I am the bread of life; whoever
comes to me will never hunger, and whoever believes
in me will never thirst."

—John 6:35

Then the two recounted what had taken place on
the way and how he was made known to them in the
breaking of the bread.

—Luke 24:35

Picking Blackberries
What will you give for a taste
of summer's last sweetness?
This jewelled crown of thorns
rings every path and highway;

No use pretending you
have not heard sweet temptation
chatter through the vines—
taste, eat

Put your hand in the thorns
and come out dripping juice,
king's purple spread from
hand to tongue.

Reach gently,
or you will find your thumb
full of thorns, and your pail
filled with unbearable tartness.

Reach gently, but reach.
The sweetest berries hide
toward the inside, hidden
beneath leaves barbed like critics.

Balance, if you must, precariously,
held by will and longing from
the net of thorns. If you want
the ripest fruit, relinquish safety.

Guard yourself only with these words:
Peril, abundance
whispered like a prayer
through purple lips.

—Lynn Ungar

In the second creation story of Genesis, God forms humans from the dust of the earth and breathes the breath of life into their nostrils. We are of the earth, formed from dust and clay. We will one day return to the earth as we are woven into the cycles of birth and death. On our life's journey we depend on and are sustained by the fruits of the earth.

Ritual meals and feasting occur in all traditions. The bread of life sustains us in all of our work and acts of love. Wheat and grapes are the eucharistic source of our communal nourishment and fruitful lives, a sacramental meal.

Sharing a meal with friends, a meal that has been lovingly made, is an experience of communion that is often as profound as what I experience in church. As Dorothy Bass writes in the introduction to *Practicing Our Faith*, "Liturgy is to daily life as consommé is to broth." Through worship we practice, in a condensed form, the awareness we are to bring to the rest of our lives. I love to cook a meal to share with others. Each week my husband and I keep Sabbath on Saturday, a day free of work and worry. Part of our ritual is to invite friends over to gather for a sacred meal and conversation. I pour love and care into each element of preparation, from shopping at our local farmer's market and co-op to chopping vegetables and marinating meat. The table is laid out with a cloth and napkins, and multi-colored wine glasses add a visual delight. Wine is poured and blessings said, but the real blessing happens in the breaking of bread together. We are nourished in both body and soul. Together we honor the gifts of the earth for our physical nourishment and the gifts of each other to nourish our souls. The sacred art of feasting invites us to savor God with all of our senses. We often hear the injunction to look and listen for God, but in a meal we get to taste, smell, and touch the sacred as well. Theologian David Ford writes some very meaningful words about the aesthetics of feasting:

> All the senses are engaged in a good feast. We taste, touch, smell, see, hear. Salvation as health is here vividly physical. Anything that heals and enhances savoring the world through our senses may feed into a salvation that culminates in feasting. From prayer for healing, and all the skills of medicine, through the accumulated wisdom of traditions of cookery, wine-making and brewing, to the experiences and habits which refine our sensual discriminations and enjoyments, the requirements for full feasting draw us deeper into appreciation of our embodiment. ("Self and Salvation: Being Transformed," 304)

Ford goes on to write that Jesus went often to meals and had a "feast-centered ethic." He turns water into wine and sits at the table with those who have been outcast. The parable of the prodigal son culminates with a grand feast in celebration of the lost son returning home again. Jesus shared a Last Supper with his disciples, a feast we repeat each week in church, and he shared bread and fish with the disciples after being resurrected.

Ford asks an important question: "As millions starve, ought anyone to be feasting?" His response is that the call is to share our food so that everyone might be fed and also to keep hope alive in God's possibilities for this world through our celebration and our inclusion of everyone at the feast.

There is a wonderful film, *Babette's Feast*, in which the title character wins some money in a lottery. She is the housekeeper for two sisters in Denmark who live an austere Christian life, and she uses the money to create a banquet for these women and their community. It is an amazing story of the power of food to nurture transformation, to break open people's hearts, and to cultivate generosity of spirit.

FOR REFLECTION

- How might our eating patterns be transformed into a sense of sacred nourishment, connecting our feasting to and honoring the land that is the source of this abundance?

- What does communion look like for you?

PRAYING WITH EARTH AS A SOURCE OF NOURISHMENT

- Plan a beautiful meal to be shared with friends. It does not have to be elaborate. Bring intention to the whole act of preparing, shopping for ingredients, cutting and dicing, cooking as a sacred act. Sit down to share the meal. Enjoy the flavors and fragrances and the way good food can nurture good conversation.

- Offer a blessing at each meal to reconnect yourself to the sacredness of food, and allow the food to nourish both your body and soul. Bring awareness to all of those involved in bringing the food to the table. Offer gratitude for the nourishment of our bodies, which sustains us in our work in the world. Practice becoming aware of the transformative nature of food to give us energy to love well.

- St. Benedict, in his Rule, wrote: "When they live by the labor of their hands, as our fathers and the apostles did, then they are really monks." We live in a time when most of us have jobs that are more mentally and emotionally demanding than physically. Is there a way you can grow some of your own food, even if just a small pot of herbs on your windowsill, as a connection to the cycle of growth that brings food to your table?

- Bake bread by hand. Read the following poem aloud as you begin, and allow its images to shape your prayer as you move through the process:

Bakerwoman God
  Bakerwoman God,
  I am your living Bread.
  Strong, brown, Bakerwoman God.
  I am your low, soft, and being-shaped loaf.

I am your rising bread,
well-kneaded by some divine and knotty pair of
    knuckles,
by your warm earth-hands.
I am bread well-kneaded.

Put me in fire, Bakerwoman God,
put me in your own bright fire.
I am warm, warm as you from fire.
I am white and gold, soft and hard, brown and round.
I am so warm from fire.

Break me, Bakerwoman God.
I am broken under your caring Word.
Drop me in your special juice in pieces.
Drop me in your blood.
Drunken me in the great red flood.
Self-giving chalice swallow me.
My skin shines in the divine wine.
My face is cup-covered and I drown.

I fall up
in a red pool
in a gold world
where your warm
sunskin hand
is there to catch
and hold me.
Bakerwoman God,
remake me.

—Alla Renée Bozarth

Our Own Earthiness

By the sweat of your face you shall eat bread until
you return to the ground, for out of it were you
taken; you are dust, and to dust you shall return.

—Genesis 3:19

We come from the earth and return to it, and so we
live in agriculture as we live in flesh. While we live
our bodies are moving particles of the earth, joined
inextricably both to the soil and to the bodies of
other living creatures.

—Wendell Berry

We praise You, Lord, for Sister Death,
from whom no one living can escape.

—St. Francis of Assisi

To be of the Earth is to know
the restlessness of being a seed
the darkness of being planted
the struggle toward the light
the pain of growth into the light
the joy of bursting and bearing fruit
the love of being food for someone
the scattering of your seeds
the decay of the seasons
the mystery of death
and the miracle of birth.

—John Soos

Ash Wednesday is a day of confronting our mortality through the symbol of ashes, beginning to strip away our comforts, and embarking on the archetypal journey into the desert that is an essential part of conversion. Conversion is the process of discovering that God is always much bigger than we imagined and that our own attempts at filling our lives with things and busyness and power look so very small in comparison. The paradox of this movement is that while we are releasing our hold on all manner of things, it may feel a bit like death.

Following the death of my mother, I returned to Seattle in those November days when the Church remembers the dead. However, I found more solace among trees than among people with well-meaning, but often trite, advice about grief. I would take long walks through my neighborhood up to Volunteer Park. First came the brilliant gold leaves of the big leaf maple, then the orange Pacific dogwood, and finally the reds of the vine maple. Then the slow process of letting go. Watching the leaves fall from the trees became a daily meditation. Some days the leaves were coaxed from their branches and released with a tentative fluttering. Other days it would seem the wind swept in and rattled the trees into letting go of their hold on life. I would walk in slow silence, the sound of the fallen, brittle leaves crumbling beneath my footsteps, taking in the beauty of this loss and wondering if I could ever find beauty in my own.

Once the last leaf had surrendered its futile grip and drifted gently to the ground, I was propelled into winter. Bare branches and days that grew shorter. The sun, when it was visible, dipped low along the horizon so that even in daytime there was a darkness that lingered and pressed upon my imagination. The walks that in autumn had provided me such solace in their beauty now in winter were times to look even more deeply for signs of life around me. Rain drizzled and doused and poured in fits and starts until finally spring came again.

Death and limitation are necessary lessons of the element of earth and the season of winter, but there is always more. From the dark soil springs forth myriad forms of creation: flowers, trees, animals, and birds; the sun returns as well, offering days that grow longer and more brilliant.

FOR REFLECTION

- What does contemplating the reality of your own mortality teach you about what is precious?

- What is your relationship to death? Have you experienced the loss of someone you love? What was its impact on your spiritual journey and practice?

PRAYING WITH EARTH AS SITE OF DEATH AND NEW LIFE

- St. Ignatius of Loyola recommended an exercise for discernment that involved contemplating your own death. When making a significant decision in your life, imagine that you are lying on your deathbed looking back on your life. From this perspective of confronting the limits of your life, which path would you have chosen? This awareness of death was recommended by many of the great Christian mystics. St. Benedict wrote in his Rule to "keep death before one's eyes daily" (4:47) as a way of heightening our sense that the choices we make matter.

- Use a piece of clay to engage in a kinesthetic meditation. Take some time to work with it in your hands, getting to know its texture. As you mold it in your hands, call to mind the Genesis creation story in which humans are formed out of clay and God breathes life into them. Contemplate what it means to be created from the earth, of dirt and dust, and then breathed into. Consider the passage from Jeremiah (Jer 18) that says God is the potter and we are the clay. As you continue to work with the clay in your hands, begin creating shapes, and notice the resistance of the material. Ponder your own way of resisting God's pressure on your life. Continue to experiment and notice what shapes want to emerge until there is one that feels like an expression of your prayer experience. When it is done, see if you can behold it without judgment, and bring a sense of wonder at this symbol—wonder at what it has to teach you about your connection to earth, wonder about a God who works with the earth to create life, wonder about the ways you resist and yield to God's touch. Take some time to journal in response to this experience.

- Honor the endings of things well. So often we brush past the end to get to the new beginning without really allowing ourselves space to grieve the losses we have experienced. When you end a job or a relationship, when you move to a new home, or when a pet dies, create a simple ritual to honor the importance those experiences have played in shaping your own longings and desires in life.

Earth's Creatures

But now ask the beasts to teach you, and the birds of
    the air to tell you;
Or the reptiles on earth to instruct you, and the fish
    of the sea to inform you.
Which of all these does not know that the hand of
    God has done this?

—Job 12:7–9

Enlarge within us the sense of
fellowship with all living things,
our brothers the animals to whom you
gave the earth as their home in
common with us.

We remember with shame that in the past
we have exercised the high dominion
of humans with ruthless cruelty
so that the voice of the earth
which should have gone up to you
in song, has been a groan of travail.

May we realize that they live not for
us alone but for themselves and for
you, and that they love the sweetness of life.

—St. Basil

It is a heart which is burning with love for the whole
of creation. . . . [Someone] who has such a heart
cannot see or call to mind a creature without [his
or her] eyes being filled with tears by reason of the
immense compassion which seizes [his or her] heart;
a heart which is softened and can no longer bear to
see or learn from others of any suffering, even the
smallest pain, being inflicted on a creature.

—St. Isaac the Syrian

Apprehend God in all things, for God is in all things.
Every single creature is full of God and is a book
about God. Every creature is a word of God. If I
spend enough time with the tiniest creature, even a
caterpillar, I would never have to prepare a sermon.
So full of God is every creature.

—Meister Eckhart

On the Feast of Epiphany in 2007, Tune arrived in our lives. She
was a nine-year-old Weimaraner who had spent her life in a breed-
ing kennel, neglected and likely abused. She was terrified that first
day we met her, shy and skittish. She broke something open in my
heart, and I knew my husband and I could give her a secure, loving
home to spend the rest of her years. She bonded to us very quickly,
claiming a place for herself on both the bed and the sofa between us,
nestling against the security of both of our bodies. But to imply that
we are the primary givers in this relationship would be very mislead-
ing. Her arrival on Epiphany is a perfect metaphor.

Adopting an older dog felt risky. Our previous dog had died just a few months prior at age ten, and I was filled with grief. Of course, love is always a risk, and as I write these words more than two years later Tune is still alive and well. My deepest hope is that we can help love her out of her fears and back into wholeness. To be cherished in this life is a gift beyond measure and one I would wish for every single living creature. To love others in such a way that they know they are already whole and beautiful is a sacred thing, perhaps the only really important thing we do in this life.

Many of us have lost sight of the tremendous gift of wisdom creatures have to offer us, simply by virtue of their "otherness." Animals don't spend their lives, as far as I know, trying to rationalize and think through things, making important plans. Their gifts of instinctual and intuitive being, love, and care invite us into a bigger way of being ourselves.

Tune reminds me daily of the essential rhythms and needs of the body: Sleep. Stretch. Play. Walk. Nap. Eat. Snuggle. There is a simplicity there that I find helpful. I grow in appreciation of the wisdom of my companion animal, who guides me in listening for the body's deepest messages and responding with love.

Theologian Andrew Linzey has written several beautiful books about animals. I am deeply moved by his service of covenanting with a companion animal. He says that it is not "our" covenant, but God's. We do not create this relationship, "rather we find ourselves placed in such by the Creator." The purpose of the covenanting liturgy is to name our responsibility for the creature in our care, encourage right relationship, and point us to the creature's theological significance—as a living example of divine grace. The service includes many beautiful biblically-based prayers and ends with a lovely expression of vows:

> I, (your name), will care for (name of your companion animal) as God's own creature.
> I will be mindful of her (or his) Christ-like vulnerability. I will love and protect her (or him) as long as she (or he) lives.
> I will be faithful and kind in both good times and bad. Amen.

Linzey writes: "People who keep animals have often made an elementary but profound discovery: animals are not machines or commodities, but beings with their own God-given lives, individuality, and personality. At their best, relationships with companion animals can help us to grow in mutuality, self-giving, and trust." He goes on to quote theologian Stephen Webb, who sees in these relationships nothing less than the self-giving of God: "Animals are more like gifts than something owned, giving us more than we expect and thus obliging us to return their gifts."

FOR REFLECTION

- What practices and gentle structures in your life would help you to honor your body's rhythms more deeply? Are there any creatures in your life to offer wisdom on this path?

PRAYING WITH EARTH AS THE HOME OF OUR FELLOW CREATURES

- Spend time with your own companion animal or out in nature asking what this creature has to teach you about God. Listen for the answer. Consider the ways the creatures in your life live fully themselves. What would it mean for you to live like this?

- Make a covenant with your companion animal (such as the one above) or write one of your own. Consider the commitment you desire to make as a reflection of the gift this creature offers to your own life.

- Take this biblical advice offered: "Go to the ant," says the book of Proverbs, "study her ways and learn wisdom" (6:6, NAB). Visit the zoo and open yourself to wonder at the diversity of creatures. Go to the park to watch squirrels or birds and see what they offer you.

Lectio Divina with Earth

Preparation

Find a place where you can contemplate the earth, perhaps in a garden or park, by a tree or in view of a mountain. You can even hold a stone in your hand or keep a plant on your altar before you. Sit so you feel comfortable, shifting your body so you are relaxed and open. Become aware of your body and the way it feels in this moment, responding to its needs. Take some time to settle into quiet. With your in-breath, breathe in an awareness of the groundedness of God; with the out-breath, breathe out all that keeps you from being fully present. With each breath imagine you have roots extending down into the ground that bring you to this moment.

Reading God's Word

Become aware of the earth before and beneath you. Notice the aspect of earth that invites you or stirs you in this time of prayer, whether a feeling, a smell, a taste, or a color. Tend to the way God might be calling you to deeper attention to earth this day. Listen until you have a sense of which dimension of earth is inviting you, and then spend some time savoring it.

Reflecting on God's Word

Continue to savor this aspect of earth, and begin to allow it to unfold in your memory and imagination and work within you to speak even more deeply. Notice what feelings, memories, or images arise for you. Allow the Spirit to expand your capacity for listening and to open you to a fuller experience of the element of earth at work in the world. Begin to notice where its qualities touch your life. What do you see, hear, touch, or remember? What is evoked in you? Allow it to interact with your thoughts, your hopes, your memories, your desires. Rest in this awareness for some time.

Responding to God's Word

After a time of resting in what the element evokes in you, you will be moved to deeper insight and a desire to respond and say yes to God. When this time comes, attend to the way the unfolding of the element connects with the context and situation of your life right now. How does it relate to what you have heard and seen this day? How does it connect with what is happening at home, at work, in your leisure time? Take an extended time of exploring this connection. How is God present to you there? Is God calling you to anything in your present circumstances? Is there a challenge presented here? Address your response to God in whatever way seems appropriate.

Resting with God's Word

Finally, simply rest in the presence of the One who has spoken to you intimately and personally through the gift of earth. Rest in the silence of God's loving embrace, and allow your heart to be moved to gratitude for this time of prayer. Allow yourself to simply be in God's rooted presence.

More Earth Quotations for Prayer

The earth is full of your loving kindness, Yahweh.

—Psalm 119:64

The vines that are tended by the Divine Gardener.

—Catherine of Siena

I want you to be a tree of love, grafted into the Word who is love, Christ crucified—a tree with its roots in deep humility. If you are a tree of love, sweetly rooted, you'll find the fruit of patience and strength at the tips of your branches, and crowned perseverance nesting within you. You'll find peace and quiet and consolation in suffering when you see yourself conformed with Christ crucified. And so, by enduring with Christ crucified, you'll come with joy from much war into much peace. Peace! Peace!

—Catherine of Siena

I live in the woods out of necessity, I get out of bed in the middle of the night because it is imperative that I hear the silence of the night, alone, and, with my face on the floor, say psalms alone, in the silence of the night . . . the silence of the forest is my bride and the sweet dark warmth of the whole world is my love and out of the heart of that dark warmth comes the secret that is only heard in silence, but it is the root of all the secrets whispered by all the lovers in their beds all over the world.

—Thomas Merton

High eternal Trinity! O Trinity, eternal Godhead! Love! We are trees of death and you are the tree of life. What a wonder, in your light, to see your creature as a pure tree, a tree you drew out of yourself, supreme purity, in pure innocence! You made this tree free, you gave it branches. But this tree became a tree of death so that it no longer produced any fruits. You engrafted your divinity into the dead tree of our humanity. O Sweet tender engrafting! So

through you who are life we will produce the fruit of
life if we choose to engraft ourselves into you.

—Catherine of Siena

I love these mountains; up here one breathes with the
pure mountain air the mysterious invitation to faith
and conversion.

—Pope John Paul II

Blessing of Earth

Spirit of the Abundant Earth,
Allow me to live in the knowledge that
I am of the earth, from the earth, and returning to the earth.

Tree of Life
Rise up in me,
Rooting me deeply in the ground
And inviting me to extend my branches far into the sky.

Spirit that rises like bread,
Knead me into the shape you desire for my life
And allow me to be nourishment for others.

Blessings of the earth be upon me.
May its taste, smell, and touch remind me of the abundance of
God.

Conclusion

I consider how God toils and labors for me in all
created things on this planet—in the heavens, the
elements, plants, fruits, flocks, and all else. He gives
existence, preserves, and makes grow.

—St. Ignatius of Loyola

All things are engaged in writing their history. The
planet, the pebble, goes attended by its shadow. The
rolling rock leaves its scratches on the mountain; the
river, its channel in the soil; the animal, its bones in
the stratum; the fern and leaf, their modest epitaph
in the coal. The falling drop makes its sculpture
in the sand or the stone. Not a foot steps into the
snow or along the ground, but prints, in characters
more or less lasting, a map of its march. Every act
of the [person] inscribes itself in the memories of its
fellows, and in his own manners and face. The air

is full of sounds, the sky of tokens, the ground is all
memoranda and signatures, and every object covered
over with hints which speak to the intelligent.

—RALPH WALDO EMERSON

Forest and field, sun and wind and sky, earth and
water, all speak the same silent language, reminding
the monk that he is here to develop like the things
that grow all around him.

—THOMAS MERTON

I write these closing words while spending some time at the
Oregon Coast. As evening falls I am witness to the fire of the sun
descending into the waters of the great Pacific Ocean. Gulls glide
on the ocean breeze, and the shore is piled with sand and stones.
Here in this place, wind, water, earth, and fire all meet in a glorious window onto the divine extravagance.

As a human species we find ourselves in a critical moment in our
relationship to the natural world. My hope is that in reading this
book, you have found resources for cultivating a contemplative relationship to nature and have discovered how much the four elements
of water, wind, earth, and fire are at the heart of the Christian tradition. They have much to teach us about the spiritual journey as
witnessed by the great poets, mystics, and sages from the last two
thousand years (and beyond in the case of the Hebrew Scriptures).
They invite us to "awaken to the natural world as the primary manifestation of the divine to human intelligence" (Thomas Berry).

Nature is the matrix through which we experience the world.
Perhaps in praying with the four elements you have glimpsed the
"inscape" of fire or wind, earth or water. *Inscape* is a term coined by
the great Jesuit poet Gerard Manley Hopkins, by which he meant
the unified complex of qualities that give each thing its own unique-
ness. God expresses God's self through fire, earth, wind, and water,
and through many other ways as well. In deepening our relationship

to the elements, we encounter the face of God. We discover unique aspects of how God works in the world.

One of the most beautiful aspects of the elements is that they ground us in kinship not only with our Christian tradition, but also even further back through time with our earliest spiritual ancestors who lived in close relationship to nature, as well as across space with our brothers and sisters from other traditions who honor the elements. Earth, wind, fire, and water are ancient and archetypal categories of the world, and as such, are containers of sacred wisdom that speak across traditions. We need only listen to receive it. We may encounter the four elements at the ocean shore at sunset, but we also contain them within our very own being: our bodies are of the earth, our blood flows through us like water, air sustains our breath, and we are enlivened by the fire of the spirit and of our own souls.

We are each called to deepen our capacity to behold the wonders of the natural world and to expand our capacity to love God's creation. This love isn't a distant, observing love, but one that calls us to enter deeply into the heart of nature and discover ourselves as an integral part.

As a closing to this volume, I offer you a prayer experience to bring together your awareness of the four elements.

Honoring the Four Elements

On an altar place a cross in the center and then a symbol of each of the elements. For example, for air you might use a feather, for fire a candle, for water a bowl with water, and for earth a stone.

WIND

Begin by facing east, the place of the rising sun, of morning, of new beginnings, and the season of springtime.

Become conscious of the element of wind: breathe in its gifts of air. Remember that the word for breath and spirit is the same in

Hebrew—*ruach*. Imagine the breath of God breathing into you at the very moment of your creation. Welcome God's life-giving breath into your life. See the dawn of creation, the birds and the winged creatures flying across the morning sky. Join them for a moment in their song, recognizing that air sustains our voices.

Notice where in your body you feel the gifts of air, breath, lightness, and the invitation to express your voice.

Ponder where in your life you feel the gift of air. Where are you being invited to greater flights of possibility? What song are you being called to sing?

With the psalmist say: "You ride on the wings of the wind" (Psalm 104).

FIRE

Turn toward the south, the place of the midday sun, the warmth and fullness of the day, and the season of summer.

Become conscious of the element of fire. Feel the heat in your own body, the energizing and expanding fire that sustains your life. Imagine the fiery tongues of the Spirit resting on the disciples at Pentecost, and welcome God's fire and passion into your life this day.

Notice in your body where you feel the gift of fire, play, warmth, and creativity burning alive. Reflect on the chemical reactions within your own cells and organs that ignite and fuel your energy, life-force, your purpose and possibility.

Ponder where in your life you feel the gift of fire. Where are you being called to a more passionate response? What sets you aflame with love?

With the psalmist say: "The voice of the Lord flashes forth flames of fire" (Psalm 29).

WATER

Turn toward the west, the place of the setting sun, of endings and transitions, and of the season of autumn.

Become conscious of the element of water. Find your pulse and feel the power of water pumping through your body, sustaining you. Imagine the power of God present in the great sea and in the cleansing and renewal of baptism. Bless yourself with water if you have some on your altar.

Notice in your body where you feel the gift and flow of water. Feel the gifts of tears, of your emotions, of the time of twilight, of letting go and turning within. Like the sun, surrendering itself at sunset, surrender yourself into the waters, or your tears, honoring the time of the turning of fall.

Ponder where in your life you feel the gift of water. Where are you being invited into a deeper surrender to the flow of life?

With the psalmist say: "Your way was through the sea, your path, through the mighty waters" (Psalm 77).

EARTH

Turn toward the north, the place of the midnight moon, a time for reflection and turning inward and the season of winter.

Become conscious of the elements of earth and the way your body is made of earth and will one day return to the earth. Imagine God as the potter and you as the clay being formed and shaped. See God as the vine and you as one of the branches extending out into the world. Experience your rootedness in the divine.

Notice in your body where you feel the gift of earth. Feel the gifts of the earth, of seeds holding wisdom underground, of roots sinking deep. Rest in your grounding and in your place on the earth. Find a few moments for introspection and solitude, listening for the wisdom of night dreams. Listen to the wisdom of the elders and the sages, those who have entered the winter of their lives.

Ponder where in your life you feel the gift of earth. Where do you need a deeper sense of grounding? Where is the call to more contemplation and resting in stillness?

With the psalmist say: "The earth is full of your goodness" (Psalm 33).

ABOVE

Reach your arms heavenward and honor the angels, saints, and ancestors, those who have traveled the path before us. Ask their blessing on the time ahead.

AROUND

Hold your arms out to your sides and honor the community across this earth of which you are a part. Remember your family and friends, pray for global issues and concerns, feel your connection to the whole of creation.

CENTER

Place your hands over your heart or in prayer position and get in touch with the still center within you. Ask for a blessing on your own dreams, longings, and desires. Open yourself to the discovery of how the Spirit is moving in your life this day.

Amen.

Sources

Introduction

E.A. van den Goorbergh and T.H. Zweerman, *Saint Francis of Assisi: A Guide for Our Times*, Leuven, Belgium: Peeters Publishers, 2007.

Thomas Merton, *The Sign of Jonas*, New York: Harcourt Brace and Company, 1953.

Ralph Waldo Emerson, *Nature and Selected Essays*, New York: Penguin, 2003.

Hannah Ward and Jennifer Wild, *The Monastic Way: Ancient Wisdom for Contemporary Living*, Grand Rapids, MI: Wm. B. Eerdmans Publishing Company, 2007.

Caitlin Matthews, *The Elements of the Celtic Tradition*, Rockport, MA: Element Books, 1989. (St. Patrick, excerpted from *Lorica*)

Joseph Ratzinger, Principles of Catholic Theology, San Francisco: Ignatius Press, 1987. (Pope Benedict XVI)

Eleanor Farjeon, "People Look East," traditional Christian hymn, 1928.

Hildegard of Bingen, *Book of Divine Works with Letters and Songs*, ed. Matthew Fox, Santa Fe, NM: Bear & Co., 1987.

Canadian Conference of Catholic Bishops, Pastoral Letter on the Christian Ecological Imperative, 2003, online at: www.cccb.ca/site/Files/ pastoralenvironment.html

Oswald Chambers, *My Utmost for His Highest*, New York: Dodd, Mead, 1935.

Chet Raymo, *Natural Prayers*, St. Paul, MN: Ruminator Books, 2000.

Thomas Becknell, *Of Earth and Sky*, Grand Rapids, MI: Augsburg Fortress Publishers, 2001.

Celtic Prayer, adapted from the Gaelic by Mary Rogers.

1. Brother Wind

St. Francis of Assisi, "The Canticle of the Creatures."

Celtic Prayer, Rogers.

Thomas Merton, *Thoughts in Solitude*, New York: Farrar, Straus and Giroux, 1999.

John of the Cross, *Selected Writings*, ed. Kieran Kavanaugh, New York: Paulist Press, 1987.

Carmen Acevedo Butcher, *Incandescence: 365 Readings with Women Mystics*, Brewster, MA: Paraclete Press, 2005. (Hildegard of Bingen, Hymn)

Eloi Leclerc, *The Canticle of Creatures: Symbols of Union*, Chicago: Franciscan Herald, 1977.

Martin Laird, *Into the Silent Land: A Guide to the Christian Practice of Contemplation*, New York: Oxford University Press, 2006. (St. Maximus the Confessor, Theophilus of Antioch, St. John of the Cross, St. John Climacus)

Ignatius of Loyola, *Spiritual Exercises and Selected Works*, ed. George Ganss, New York: Paulist Press, 1991.

Hildegard of Bingen, *Book of Divine Works with Letters and Songs*.

Conrad DeMeester, *With Empty Hands: The Spirituality of Thérèse of Lisieux*, New York: Burns & Oates, 2002.

Morton D. Paley, *The Traveller in the Evening: The Last Works of William Blake*, New York: Oxford University Press, 2008.

Mechtild of Magdeburg, *The Flowing Light of the Godhead*, ed. Frank Tobin, New York: Paulist Press, 1997.

Hildegard of Bingen, Letter to Pope Eugene III.

Shawn Madigan, *Mystics, Visionaries, and Prophets: A Historical Anthology of Women's Spiritual Writings*, Minneapolis: Fortress Press, 2004. (St. Gertrude the Great, *The Herald of Divine Love*)

Thomas Merton, *New Seeds of Contemplation*, Norfolk, CT: New Directions, 2007.

David Whyte, "What to Remember When Waking," in *House of Belonging*, Langley, WA; Many Rivers Press, 1996.

Gail Ramshaw, *Treasures Old and New: Images in the Lectionary*, Minneapolis: Augsburg Fortress Publishers, 2002. (Origen, *The Testing of the Apostles*)

Mechtild of Magdeburg, *Flowing Light of the Godhead.*

Hildegard of Bingen, *Book of Divine Works.*

Marguerite Porete, *The Mirror of Simple Souls*, ed. Ellen Babinsky, New York: Paulist Press, 1993.

Meister Eckhart, *The Sermons and Collations of Meister Eckhart*, ed. Franz Pfeiffer, Belle Fourche, SD: Kessinger Publishing, 1992.

Samuel Taylor Coleridge, *Rime of the Ancient Mariner*, Charleston, SC: Forgotten Books, 2008.

Butcher, *Incandescence.* (Hildegard of Bingen, Hymn)

Pierre Teilhard de Chardin, *The Hymn of the Universe*, New York: Harper & Row, 1965.

2. Brother Fire

St. Francis of Assisi, "The Canticle of the Creatures."

Celtic Prayer, Rogers.

Gerard Manley Hopkins, "God's Grandeur" from *Gerard Manley Hopkins: The Major Works*, ed. Catherine Philips, Oxford: Oxford University Press, 2009.

Annie Dillard, *Pilgrim at Tinker Creek*, New York: Harper Perennial Modern Classics, 2007.

Thomas Merton, "In Silence" from *In the Dark Before Dawn: New Selected Poems of Thomas Merton*, New York: New Directions Publishing, 2005.

Mechtild of Magdeburg, *Flowing Light of the Godhead.*

Alla Renée Bozarth, "Where Life Begins," *From Reading Out Loud to God*, audiocassette, Wisdom House, 1990; *At the Foot of the Mountain: Nature and the Art of Soul Healing*, iUniverse, 2000; *This is My Body ~ Praying for Earth, Prayers from the Heart*, iUniverse, 2004. All rights reserved. For reprint permission contact Alla Bozarth, Wisdom House, 43222 SE Tapp. Rd., Sandy, OR 97055, tel. 503-668-3119 or allabearheart@yahoo.com.

Mechtild of Magdeburg, *Flowing Light of the Godhead.*

Madigan, *Mystics, Visionaries, and Prophets.* (St. Gertrude the Great, *The Herald of Divine Love*)

St. Gregory the Great, *The Life and Miracles of Saint Benedict*, New York: Cosimo Classics, 2007.

Peter Mayer, Excerpted song lyrics from "O Sun" © Peter Mayer www .blueboat .net, used by permission of the artist.

Gail Ramshaw, *Treasures Old and New: Images in the Lectionary*, Minneapolis: Augsburg Fortress Publishers, 2002. (The Exsultet [Easter Proclamation])

Thomas Merton, *Thomas Merton: Spiritual Master*, ed. Lawrence Cunningham, New York: Paulist Press, 1992.

G.E.H. Palmer, Philip Sherrard, and Kallistos Ware, trans., *The Philokalia, Volume 4: The Complete Text*, compiled by St. Nikodimos of the Holy Mountain and St. Markarios of Corinth, London: Faber & Faber, 1999. (Gregory Palamas)

Hildegard of Bingen, *Book of Divine Works*.

Sigurd F. Olson, *Reflections from the North Country*, New York: Knopf, 1976.

Catherine of Siena, *The Dialogue*, eds. Suzanne Noffke and Giuliana Cavallini, New York: Paulist Press, 1980.

Lucien Stryk and Takashi Ikemoto, *Zen Poetry: Let the Spring Breeze Enter*, New York: Grove Press, 1995. (Masahide)

Tim Vivian, ed., *Becoming Fire: Through the Year with the Desert Fathers and Mothers*, Trappist, KY: Cistercian Publications, 2008. (Desert Fathers)

Mechtild of Magdeburg, *Flowing Light of the Godhead*.

Madigan, *Mystics, Visionaries, and Prophets*. (St. Gertrude the Great, *The Herald of Divine Love*)

Alan G. McDougall, *Thoughts of St. Ignatius of Loyola for Every Day of the Year*, trans. Patrick J. Ryan, New York: Fordham University Press, 2006. (St. Ignatius of Loyola)

St. John of the Cross, *Selected Writings*.

Pierre Teilhard de Chardin, *The Divine Milieu*, New York: Harper & Row, 1960.

Mechtild of Magdeburg, *Flowing Light of the Godhead*.

Hildegard of Bingen, *Book of Divine Works*.

Ramshaw, *Treasures Old and New*. (St. Ambrose of Milan)

Chet Raymo, *Soul of the Night: An Astronomical Pilgrimage*. Englewood Cliffs, NJ: Cowley Publications, 2005.

Peter London, *Drawing Closer to Nature: Making Art in Dialogue with the Natural World*, Boston: Shambhala, 2003.

Christopher Uhl, *Developing Ecological Consciousness: Path to a Sustainable Future*, Lanham, MD: Rowman & Littlefield Publishers, 2003.

Butcher, *Incandescence*. (Hildegard of Bingen, Hymn)

Dillard, *Pilgrim at Tinker Creek*.

Thomas Merton, *Conjectures of a Guilty Bystander*, Garden City, NY: Image, 1968.

C. S. Lewis, *The Magician's Nephew*, New York: HarperCollins, 2003.

3. Sister Water

St. Francis of Assisi, "Canticle of the Creatures."

Celtic Prayers, Rogers.

Mechtild of Magdeburg, *The Flowing Light of the Godhead.*

Butcher, *Incandescence.* (St. Gertrude the Great, Hymn of Thanksgiving, *Spiritual Exercises*)

Madigan, *Mystics, Visionaries, and Prophets.* (Catherine of Siena, *The Dialogue*)

Peter Mayer, Excerpted song lyrics from "God is a River" © Peter Mayer www .blueboat.net, used by permission of the artist.

Herman Melville, *Moby Dick.*

Prayer attributed to St. Aidan of Lindisfarne.

Rainer Maria Rilke, "Ich glaube an Alles. . ./I believe in all that has never yet been spoken," from *Rilke's Book of Hours: Love Poems to God,* translated by Anita Barrows and Joanna Macy, copyright © 1996 by Anita Barrows and Joanna Macy. Used by permission of Riverhead Books, an imprint of Penguin Group (USA) Inc.

George Willis Cooke, *Ralph Waldo Emerson: His Life, Writings, and Philosophy,* Boston: J. R. Osgood, 1881.

Rachel Carson, *The Edge of the Sea,* Boston: Houghton Mifflin, 1955.

John O'Donohue, *Anam Cara: A Book of Celtic Wisdom,* New York: Harper Perennial, 2004.

Anne Morrow Lindbergh, *Gift from the Sea,* New York: Pantheon, 1991.

Butcher, *Incandescence.* (Catherine of Siena, *Letters*)

Thomas Merton, *The Collected Poems of Thomas Merton,* New York: New Directions Publishing, 1980.

Butcher, *Incandescence.* (St. Gertrude the Great)

Denise Levertov, "The Fountain," from *Poems: 1960–1967,* New York: New Directions Publishing, 1983. Copyright ©1961 by Denise Levertov. Reprinted by permission of New Directions Publishing Corp.

Attributed to Hildegard of Bingen.

Hildegard of Bingen, "Sequence for the Holy Spirit."

Thomas Merton, "Rain and the Rhinoceros," from *Raids on the Unspeakable,* New York: New Directions Publishing, 1966.

Traditional Eastern Orthodox *Sticheron* or "Hymn." (Hymn of the Great Blessing of Waters)

Dillard, *Pilgrim at Tinker Creek.*

St. Augustine of Hippo, *The City of God.*

Hildegard of Bingen, *Book of Divine Works.*

4. Sister Earth

St. Francis of Assisi, "The Canticle of the Creatures."

Celtic Prayer, Rogers.

William Stafford, *A Scripture of Leaves.* Elgin, IL: Brethren Press 1989.

Thomas Merton, "O Earth! O Earth! When will we hear you sing . . .?" from *Entering the Silence: The Journals of Thomas Merton, Volume Two 1941–1952* by Thomas Merton and edited by Jonathan Montaldo. Copyright ©1995 by The Merton Legacy Trust. Reprinted by permission of HarperCollins publishers.

Madigan, *Mystics, Visionaries, and Prophets.* (Catherine of Siena)

Gerard Manley Hopkins, "Pied Beauty," from *The Major Works.*

Fyodor Dostoevsky, *The Brothers Karamazov.*

Joseph Campbell, *The Power of Myth*, New York: Doubleday, 1991.

London, *Drawing Closer to Nature.*

St. Bonaventure, *The Soul's Journey into God, the Tree of Life, the Life of St. Francis*, ed. Ewert Cousins, New York: Paulist Press, 1978.

St. Gertrude the Great, *The Herald of Divine Love.*

Rainer Maria Rilke, "Wenn etwas mir vom Fenster Fallt. . ./How surely gravity's law," from *Rilke's Book of Hours: Love Poems to God* by Rainer Maria Rilke, translated by Anita Barrows and Joanna Macy, copyright © 1996 by Anita Barrows and Joanna Macy. Used by permission of Riverhead Books, an imprint of Penguin Group (USA) Inc.

Colin Tudge, *The Secret Life of Trees: How They Live and Why They Matter*, London: Penguin, 2006.

Pope John Paul II, cited at http://conservation.catholic.org/pope_john_paul_ii.htm

Annie Dillard, *Holy the Firm*, New York: Harper Perennial, 1988.

Merton, *New Seeds of Contemplation.*

Hildegard of Bingen, *Book of Divine Works.*

Tim Robinson, *Setting Foot on the Shores of Connemara*, Dublin: Lilliput Press, 1996.

Vigen Guroian, *Fragrance of God*, Grand Rapids, MI: Wm. B. Eerdmans Publishing Company, 2006.

St. Thérèse of Lisieux, *Story of a Soul*, Washington: ICS Publications, 1996.

Lynn Ungar, "Picking Blackberries," from *Blessing the Bread: Meditations*, Boston: Skinner House Books, 1995. © Lynn Ungar, used by permission of the poet.

Dorothy Bass, ed., *Practicing Our Faith: A Way of Life for a Searching People*, San Francisco, CA: Jossey-Bass, 1998.

David Ford, "Self and Salvation: Being Transformed," from *Theological Aesthetics: A Reader*, Grand Rapids, MI: Wm. B. Eerdmans Publishing Company, 2005.

Alla Renée Bozarth, "Bakerwoman God," from *Water Women*, audiocassette, Wisdom House, 1990; *Womanpriest: A Personal Odyssey*, Luramedia, 1988, Wisdom House dist.; *This is My Body ~ Praying for Earth, Prayers from the Heart*, iUniverse, 2004. All rights reserved. For reprint permission contact Alla Bozarth, Wisdom House, 43222 SE Tapp. Rd., Sandy, OR 97055, tel. 503-668-3119 or allabearheart@yahoo.com.

Wendell Berry, "The Body and the Earth," from *The Art of the Commonplace*. Washington, D.C.: Counterpoint, 2002.

St. Francis of Assisi, "The Canticle of the Creatures."

Elizabeth Roberts, ed., *Earth Prayers from Around the World: 365 Prayers, Poems, and Invocations for Honoring the Earth*, San Francisco: HarperOne, 1991. (John Soos)

Andrew Linzey, *Animal Theology*, Urbana, IL: University of Illinois Press, 1995. (St. Basil and St. Isaac the Syrian)

Matthew Fox, ed., *Meditations with Meister Eckhart*, Santa Fe, NM: Bear & Company, 1983.

Andrew Linzey, *Animal Rites: Liturgies of Animal Care*, Valley Forge, PA: Trinity Press International, 2000.

Madigan, *Mystics, Visionaries, and Prophets*. (Catherine of Siena)

Butcher, *Incandescence*. (Catherine of Siena, *Letters*)

Thomas Merton, *Dancing in the Water of Life: Seeking Peace in the Hermitage*, New York: Harper Collins, 1997.

Madigan, *Mystics, Visionaries, and Prophets*. (Catherine of Siena, *Letters*)

Pope John Paul II, Vacationing in the Italian Alps, 1990.

Conclusion

St. Ignatius of Loyola, *Spiritual Exercises and Selected Works*.

The Complete Works of Ralph Waldo Emerson, Boston: Houghton Mifflin, 1903.

Thomas Merton, *The Waters of Siloe*, New York: Harvest Books, 1979.

Thomas Berry, from the Foreword to Thomas Merton's, *When the Trees Say Nothing: Writings on Nature*, ed. Kathleen Deignan, Notre Dame, IN: Sorin Books, 2003.

Christine Valters Paintner serves as the Program Coordinator for the Ignatian Spirituality Center in Seattle and is also adjunct faculty at Seattle University's School of Theology and Ministry. Paintner is a Benedictine Oblate and serves as Art Editor for *Presence: An International Journal of Spiritual Direction*.